The First Men in Space

WORLD EXPLORERS

The First Men in Space

Gregory P. Kennedy

Introductory Essay by Michael Collins

CHELSEA HOUSE PUBLISHERS

New York · Philadelphia

On the cover View of the earth from the Gemini XII capsule; portraits of Yury Gagarin, Alan Shepard, and John Glenn.

Chelsea House Publishers
Editor-in-Chief Remmel Nunn
Managing Editor Karyn Gullen Browne
Copy Chief Juliann Barbato
Picture Editor Adrian G. Allen
Art Director Maria Epes
Deputy Copy Chief Mark Rifkin
Assistant Art Director Noreen Romano
Series Design Loraine Machlin
Manufacturing Manager Gerald Levine
Systems Manager Lindsey Ottman
Production Manager Joseph Romano
Production Coordinator Marie Claire Cebrián

World Explorers
Senior Editor Sean Dolan

Staff for THE FIRST MEN IN SPACE
Associate Editor Terrance Dolan
Copy Editor Karen Hammonds
Editorial Assistant Martin Mooney
Picture Researcher Nisa Rauschenberg
Senior Designer Basia Niemczyc

7   9   8   6

Library of Congress Cataloging-in-Publication Data

Kennedy, Gregory P.
The first men in space / Gregory P. Kennedy.
p.   cm.—(World explorers)
Includes bibliographical references and index.
Summary: Examines the early days of space exploration.
ISBN 0-7910-1324-3
       0-7910-1548-3 (pbk.)
1. Outer space—Exploration—Juvenile literature. [1. Outer
space—Exploration.] I. Title. II. Series.   90-2258
TL793.K44 1990   CIP
629.45—dc20   AC

CONTENTS

WORLD EXPLORERS

CHELSEA HOUSE PUBLISHERS

Into the Unknown

Michael Collins

It is difficult to define most eras in history with any pre-cision, but not so the space age. On October 4, 1957, it burst on us with little warning when the Soviet Union launched *Sputnik*, a 184-pound cannonball that circled the globe once every 96 minutes. Less than 4 years later, the Soviets followed this first primitive satellite with the flight of Yury Gagarin, a 27-year-old fighter pilot who became the first human to orbit the earth. The Soviet Union's success prompted President John F. Kennedy to decide that the United States should "land a man on the moon and return him safely to earth" before the end of the 1960s. We now had not only a space age but a space race.

I was born in 1930, exactly the right time to allow me to participate in Project Apollo, as the U.S. lunar program came to be known. As a young man growing up, I often found myself too young to do the things I wanted—or suddenly too old, as if someone had turned a switch at midnight. But for Apollo, 1930 was the perfect year to be born, and I was very lucky. In 1966 I enjoyed circling the earth for three days, and in 1969 I flew to the moon and laughed at the sight of the tiny earth, which I could cover with my thumbnail.

How the early explorers would have loved the view from space! With one glance Christopher Columbus could have plotted his course and reassured his crew that the world was indeed round. In 90 minutes Magellan could have looked down at every port of call in the *Victoria*'s three-year circumnavigation of the globe. Given a chance to map their route from orbit, Lewis and Clark could have told President Jefferson that there was no easy Northwest Passage but that a continent of exquisite diversity awaited their scrutiny.

In a physical sense, we have already gone to most places that we can. That is not to say that there are not new adventures awaiting us deep in the sea or on the red plains of Mars, but more important than reaching new places will be understanding those we have already visited. There are vital gaps in our understanding of how our planet works as an ecosystem and how our planet fits into the infinite order of the universe. The next great age may well be the age of assimilation, in which we use microscope and telescope to evaluate what we have discovered and put that knowledge to use. The adventure of being first to reach may be replaced by the satisfaction of being first to grasp. Surely that is a form of exploration as vital to our well-being, and perhaps even survival, as the distinction of being the first to explore a specific geographical area.

The explorers whose stories are told in the books of this series did not just sail perilous seas, scale rugged mountains, traverse blistering deserts, dive to the depths of the ocean, or land on the moon. Their voyages and expeditions were journeys of mind as much as of time and distance, through which they—and all of mankind—were able to reach a greater understanding of our universe. That challenge remains, for all of us. The imperative is to see, to understand, to develop knowledge that others can use, to help nurture this planet that sustains us all. Perhaps being born in 1975 will be as lucky for a new generation of explorer as being born in 1930 was for Neil Armstrong, Buzz Aldrin, and Mike Collins.

The Reader's Journey

William H. Goetzmann

This volume is one of a series that takes us with the great explorers of the ages on bold journeys over the oceans and the continents and into outer space. As we travel along with these imaginative and courageous journeyers, we share their adventures and their knowledge. We also get a glimpse of that mysterious and inextinguishable fire that burned in the breast of men such as Magellan and Columbus—the fire that has propelled all those throughout the ages who have been driven to leave behind family and friends for a voyage into the unknown.

No one has ever satisfactorily explained the urge to explore, the drive to go to the "back of beyond." It is certain that it has been present in man almost since he began walking erect and first ventured across the African savannas. Sparks from that same fire fueled the transoceanic explorers of the Ice Age, who led their people across the vast plain that formed a land bridge between Asia and North America, and the astronauts and scientists who determined that man must reach the moon.

Besides an element of adventure, all exploration involves an element of mystery. We must not confuse exploration with discovery. Exploration is a purposeful human activity—a search for something. Discovery may be the end result of that search; it may also be an accident, as when Columbus found a whole new world while searching for the Indies. Often, the explorer may not even realize the full significance of what he has discovered, as was the case with Columbus. Exploration, on the other hand, is the product of a cultural or individual curiosity; it is a unique process that has enabled mankind to know and understand the world's oceans, continents, and polar regions. It is at the heart of scientific thinking. One of its most significant aspects is that it teaches people to ask the right questions; by doing so, it forces us to reevaluate what we think we know and understand. Thus knowledge progresses, and we are driven constantly to a new awareness and appreciation of the universe in all its infinite variety.

The motivation for exploration is not always pure. In his fascination with the new, man often forgets that others have been there before him. For example, the popular notion of the discovery of America overlooks the complex Indian civilizations that had existed there for thousands of years before the arrival of Europeans. Man's desire for conquest, riches, and fame is often linked inextricably with his quest for the unknown, but a story that touches so closely on the human essence must of necessity treat war as well as peace, avarice with generosity, both pride and humility, frailty and greatness. The story of exploration is above all a story of humanity and of man's understanding of his place in the universe.

The WORLD EXPLORERS series has been divided into four sections. The first treats the explorers of the ancient world, the Viking explorers of the 9th through the 11th centuries, and Marco Polo and the medieval explorers. The rest of the series is divided into three great ages of exploration. The first is the era of Columbus and Magellan: the period spanning the 15th and 16th centuries, which saw the discovery and exploration of the New World and the world ocean. The second might be called the age of science and imperialism, the era made possible by the scientific advances of the 17th century, which witnessed the discovery of the world's last two undiscovered continents, Australia and Antarctica, the mapping of all the continents and oceans, and the establishment of colonies all over the world. The third great age refers to the most ambitious quests of the 20th century—the probing of space and of the ocean's depths.

As we reach out into the darkness of outer space and other galaxies, we come to better understand how our ancestors confronted *oecumene,* or the vast earthly unknown. We learn once again the meaning of an unknown 18th-century sea captain's advice to navigators:

> And if by chance you make a landfall on the shores of another sea in a far country inhabited by savages and barbarians, remember you this: the greatest danger and the surest hope lies not with fires and arrows but in the quicksilver hearts of men.

At its core, exploration is a series of moral dramas. But it is these dramas, involving new lands, new people, and exotic ecosystems of staggering beauty, that make the explorers' stories not only moral tales but also some of the greatest adventure stories ever recorded. They represent the process of learning in its most expansive and vivid forms. We see that real life, past and present, transcends even the adventures of the starship *Enterprise.*

"By the Light of a Communist Moon"

For many of the inhabitants of this small planet, the space age began on the evening of October 4, 1957, when the Soviet Union successfully launched and put into orbit *Sputnik 1*, the first artificial earth satellite. The launching of *Sputnik 1* had a profound impact on Americans especially; the cold war was escalating, and the small, crude metallic cylinder, passing unseen above the atmosphere, became an object of menace and a cause for paranoia. The mysterious orb was known to Americans simply as *Sputnik*, and the name evoked images of an omniscient, unblinking Communist eye, circling the earth and gazing balefully down on the exposed lives of the citizens of the "free world." There was the unnerving sensation of being watched; Americans were sure that *Sputnik* was a spying device and they began to feel like insects under some all-seeing Soviet microscope. The skies, in the words of Texas senator and later U.S. president Lyndon B. Johnson, now seemed to be "almost alien." Johnson went on to describe the "shock of realizing that it might be possible for another nation to achieve technological superiority over this great country of ours." And if the Russians could put a satellite into orbit, how long would it be before some kind of manned Soviet spacecraft was circling the earth as well? It seemed conceivable, and even possible, that the Communists might soon take control of the skies and even put a man on the moon. "I, for one," Johnson declared, "don't want to go to bed by the light of a communist moon."

Sputnik 1, *the first artificial earth satellite, was launched on October 4, 1957, by the Soviet Union. The launching of* Sputnik 1 *signaled the beginning of the space race and the start of an era that would see outer space become a cold war arena.*

*Explorers of the new frontier:
From left to right are Soviet
cosmonauts Yury Gagarin,
Gherman Titov, Valentina
Tereshkova, Adrian Nikolayev,
and Pavel Popovich.*

Inevitably, then, with the dawning of the space age came the start of the space race—an ongoing competition between the United States and the Soviet Union to explore outer space. In pre-Glasnost times, it was hard to divorce the beginning of manned space exploration from the politics that seemed to have generated it, but it is clear in retrospect that politics only provided the excuse for the two superpowers to begin marshaling the vast resources needed to put a human in space. The hunger, the need, the urge to *go up*, was there from the first time a human being gazed at the stars and the moon shining in the night sky. If the competitive edge provided by the cold war is removed—the instinct to claim, to occupy, to colonize, to annex—the initial goals of manned space exploration were the same as they are for any journey of exploration: to get there, take a look around, get home safely, and then tell everyone else about it.

But if the essence of space exploration had much in common with the exploration of earth that came first, there was also much about the extraterrestrial journey that was unique. Creaking, windblown wooden ships were replaced by thunderous, fiery missiles and oddly shaped modules and capsules; the powers of the winds and ocean currents were replaced by the gravitational attraction of moons and planets. And the success or failure of a mission now seemed to rest more on science and technology than on the capacity of individuals for endurance and their will to survive. This emphasis on technology produced some of the most profound changes in the nature of exploration for it entailed the participation of unprecedented numbers of people, each of whom played an essential part in the

Astronaut M. Scott Carpenter studies a celestial globe prior to his historic spaceflight aboard the Aurora 7 *in May 1962. Like the terrestrial explorers who came before them, astronauts—and their computers—depend on the stars for navigation.*

Apollo 11 astronaut Buzz Aldrin poses for a photograph on the surface of the moon, July 20, 1969. Fellow astronaut Neil Armstrong used a specially developed lunar-surface camera to take the photo. Armstrong's reflection can be seen in Aldrin's visor.

journey. Christopher Columbus sailed to the New World with the help of royal funds, certain shipbuilders, the designers of navigation instruments, a few limited maps, and his crew; America's Mercury, Gemini, and Apollo astronauts were propelled into space by the combined efforts of an entire nation, and the same was true, to a certain extent, of the Soviet space effort. Everyone from factory assembly-line workers to astrophysics theoreticians got involved. As writer Richard S. Lewis put it in his history of exploration, *From Vinland to Mars*, the astronauts "formed the apex of a social pyramid comprising the scientific, technical, and industrial power of a whole society."

Technology provided another medium of mass participation that made space exploration unique. Radio, and then television, allowed entire countries, and indeed the entire world, eventually, to go along on the journeys of the astronauts and cosmonauts. Even before televised spaceflight began, communications technology provided a new and dramatic sense of immediacy. In the minutes leading up to the launch of the first manned American flight, cars and trucks pulled off roads and highways across America and came to a stop as drivers sought to concentrate on the countdown over the radio. Those on the earth could share, with their eyes and ears and hearts, the space explorers' triumphs (the sight of Neil Armstrong stepping onto the surface of the moon and the sound of his voice as he uttered his famous words) and also their tragedies (the sight of the space shuttle *Challenger* exploding and the flaming debris falling back to earth). Imagine if Magellan or Columbus had had radio or television.

However, the collective nature of space exploration can be overemphasized, for at the crux of every journey into space are the astronauts and cosmonauts. These men and woman, the explorers, are the same as all the terrestrial explorers who preceded them—pathfinders with an insatiable appetite to go first and to see first. And death, as it has been since the first days of exploration, is a constant companion of the space explorers, dogging their footsteps or contrails from beginning to end. To death by drowning or freezing or starving has now been added the possibility of death by exposure to the freezing void of outer space, or death by loss of oxygen to breathe, or death by impact with the earth's atmosphere or the earth itself, or death by lack of enough fuel to return to earth—no death more chilling and lonely can be found at the earth's poles or beneath its seas. And there is always the threat of death by fire. During almost every manned Mercury, Gemini, Vostok, or Voskhod flight, there came that crucial moment when the success of the mission and the survival of the explorers depended upon the resourcefulness and courage of the astronaut or cosmonaut. The decisions that had to be made at these moments were of a more technical nature than those faced by Magellan or Peary—to flick a switch or not to flick a switch—but they were life-and-death decisions nevertheless. The participation of the earthbound technician at mission control during spaceflight cannot be ignored; the importance of the NASA bureaucrats to the success of the space effort cannot be ignored, either; but if something goes wrong during a flight, these people still return safely to their homes and families, whereas the astronaut or cosmonaut does not.

As *Sputnik* began its first orbit of the earth on that autumn night in 1957, it sounded the bell for the start of a new round in the cold war. But more important, it signaled the beginning of a new age of exploration, and the coming of some of the most thrilling events in the history of the human race. *Sputnik*, that most political of celestial objects, was actually the harbinger of an endeavor the very nature of which renders politics insignificant. For, whether they bore Soviet or American insignia; whether Mercury or Vostok; whether they were piloted by astronaut Alan Shepard or cosmonaut Yury Gagarin, the spacecraft that followed *Sputnik* were all part of the beginning of the greatest chapter in the history of the human odyssey.

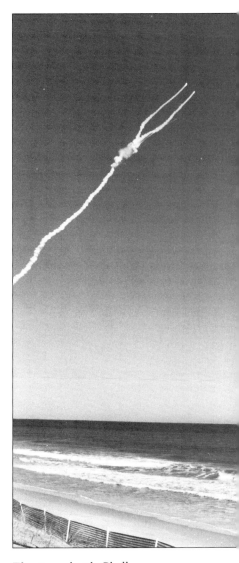

The space shuttle Challenger *explodes moments after takeoff on January 28, 1986. This photograph was taken by a resident of Satellite Beach, Florida—one of thousands who gathered on the beaches near Cape Kennedy to watch the launch.*

"Ordinary Supermen"

The U.S. space program started in much the same way as the Soviet program: Following World War II, both Soviet and American scientists began experiments with rockets captured from the defeated Nazi Germany, particularly the long-range missile known as the Vengeance Weapon-2, or V-2. The concept of space travel through the use of liquid propellant rockets had been explored before World War II, primarily by the Russian Konstantin Tsiolkovsky, who published his *Exploration of Cosmic Space with Reactive Devices* in 1911; Germans Hermann Oberth, who published several books on the subject between 1923 and 1928, and Wernher von Braun, a disciple of Oberth's who launched small rockets from a Berlin suburb in 1930 and went on to play a leading role in the development of the V-2; and the American Robert Goddard, who launched the world's first liquid propellant rocket from his aunt's Massachusetts cabbage patch in March 1926. It was not until after World War II, however, when the cold-war rivalry generated a contest to see which nation could put a man in space first, that the two superpowers began any kind of serious effort to realize the concept of space travel. The Soviet space program grew up under the guiding hand of the legendary—and for Americans, mysterious—Chief Designer Sergey Korolyov. Korolyov had been involved in rocket research since the

Pioneering rocket scientist Robert H. Goddard in his Roswell, New Mexico, laboratory. Goddard (1882–1945) first considered the possibilities of spaceflight at the age of 16 after reading a science fiction story about interplanetary travel. Goddard launched the world's first liquid propellant rocket in 1926; it achieved an altitude of 41 feet.

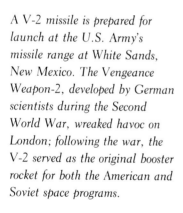

A V-2 missile is prepared for launch at the U.S. Army's missile range at White Sands, New Mexico. The Vengeance Weapon-2, developed by German scientists during the Second World War, wreaked havoc on London; following the war, the V-2 served as the original booster rocket for both the American and Soviet space programs.

early 1930s, had survived Stalin's purges, and emerged as head of the post–World War II space program. In the United States, similar research was undertaken after the war by various government agencies and branches of the armed forces, including the National Advisory Committee for Aeronautics (NACA). One of the most important and influential members of the U.S. effort was none other than Wernher von Braun, who, along with 127 other German rocket scientists, had fled Germany and come to America following the fall of the Third Reich.

Both the Soviet and American space programs spent the late forties and early to mid-fifties trying to answer the major questions that were raised concerning the concept of sending a human being beyond the earth's atmosphere. How might a person respond to the weightlessness that would occur when a spacecraft escaped the earth's gravity? What effects would the tremendous acceleration needed to break free of the earth's atmosphere have on the human body? Could a person function capably over a sustained period while isolated and confined within a tiny capsule? Could a life-support system be built that was reliable enough to sustain humans for hours or days in the hostile, unforgiving void of outer space? And how would the human psyche react to this environment? There were a host

Wernher von Braun (1912–77), born in Wirsitz, Germany, was the man most responsible for the development of the V-2. Following the fall of the German Reich, von Braun and 127 of his associates found asylum in the United States, where they were instrumental to the success of the fledgling American space program. Von Braun was named deputy associate administrator of NASA in 1970.

of other unknowns, including questions regarding the hazards posed by solar and cosmic (deep-space) radiation.

These questions led to the first biological rocket flights; before any humans ventured into space, animals paved the way. Dogs, mice, monkeys, chimps, rabbits, and frogs, along with various forms of plant and vegetable life, rode rockets into space. The first attempted flight of a mammal occurred on June 11, 1948, when Dr. James P. Henry and Captain David G. Simons, both physicians at the Air Force Aeromedical Laboratory at Wright Field, Ohio (today, Wright Patterson Air Force Base), placed a rhesus monkey named Albert aboard a V-2. Albert's respiration and pulse rate were monitored on the ground. There was no indication of either heart action or respiration during the 39-mile-high flight, so Henry and Simons concluded that Albert died prior to lift-off. In any event, Albert would

The famed chief designer of the Soviet Union's space program, Sergey Korolyov, at the Baikonur Cosmodrome in 1961, shortly before the launch of Vostok 1, *the first manned spacecraft. Korolyov dominated the first years of the space race.*

have died upon landing, for the parachute failed. After numerous failures of this sort, the first live recovery was achieved at the White Sands Proving Grounds, in New Mexico, on September 20, 1951. After carrying a rhesus monkey and 11 mice to 236,000 feet, a new model of rocket called the Aerobee returned to earth with all passengers intact. (Unfortunately, the monkey died of heat prostration about two hours later.)

In the Soviet Union, similar—but more successful—experiments were under way. In 1951, Sergey Korolyov placed two dogs aboard a modified V-2. Both animals were

Dr. James P. Henry (left) and Colonel Edwin R. Ballinger of the Wright Air Development Center, Dayton, Ohio, with two of the first earthlings to travel into the stratosphere. The 2 monkeys flew aboard an Aerobee rocket to an altitude of 37 miles and returned to earth with no adverse symptoms.

Monkey Baker, the intrepid squirrel monkey who rode in the nose cone of an American Jupiter rocket in May 1959. While animals were being exposed to high-altitude conditions aboard rockets, human passengers were reaching significant heights in balloons.

recovered alive after reaching an altitude of more than 60 miles. By 1955, the chief designer's animals were wearing space suits and helmets, traveling in unpressurized capsules, and ejecting from the rockets and returning to terra firma via individual parachutes following the flight. These flights would be particularly important to later Soviet missions, for they tested what was to become the standard Soviet return technique.

American researchers eventually came to believe that up-and-down rocket flights did not provide enough exposure time to determine the long-term effects of high-altitude travel. Balloons, which were capable of reaching and sustaining extreme altitudes, seemed to provide a much better vehicle for this type of research. While biological rocket flights continued with the Jupiter program, balloons carrying small animals, insects, film packages, and tissue samples were sent aloft to determine the effects of sustained exposure to cosmic and solar radiation. In 1957, Project Manhigh placed a human passenger in a pressurized capsule attached to a high-altitude balloon that ascended to 100,000 feet. At such an altitude, the capsule was above most of the atmosphere and in the equivalent of an outer-space environment. Project Manhigh continued for almost four years and yielded valuable data concerning radiation exposure and the effects of isolation and confinement on human passengers.

The launching of *Sputnik 1* in 1957 changed everything; it was, for the United States, the first great defeat in the cold war. Galvanized by the news of the success of the Soviet satellite, the U.S. government joined the space race in earnest and initiated a concerted national effort to put an American in space. In July 1958, Congress passed the National Aeronautics and Space Act, thus creating the National Aeronautics and Space Administration (NASA). NASA absorbed NACA; lunar programs from the army and air force; air force rocket engine programs; the navy's Vanguard scientific satellite program; and (eventually) part of the Army Ballistic Missile Agency. On October 7, 1958, NASA officially announced the establishment of a national manned spaceflight project. NASA's director of spaceflight development, Abe Silverstein, suggested the project be named Mercury, after the messenger of the Roman gods. At about the same time, Korolyov received authorization to proceed with his own plan to put a man in orbit. The Soviet project was named Vostok (East). Now both the U.S. and Soviet space programs were faced with the all-important task of choosing the pilots for the proposed missions.

In many ways, this was the most difficult problem encountered by the chief designer and his American counterparts, for it was here that the human element came into play. Technical problems were one thing—engineers could always straighten them out—but the always unpredictable human element was a different matter altogether. In the end, the success of the missions would depend on the physical and psychological makeup of the pilots. What criteria should be used to choose the pilots? Individuals with an extraordinary combination of physical prowess, psychological stability, and intellectual capabilities, not to mention courage, were needed. "What we're looking for," one air force general remarked, "is a group of ordinary supermen." Some in the United States favored selecting persons who had experience as arctic or antarctic explorers or as submarine crew members. Presumably, these people would be better able to cope with the isolation and constant threat of crisis expected during space travel. Still others favored selecting persons with parachuting, race-car driving, mountain-climbing, or deep-sea-diving experience. Eventually, the Mercury planners decided to search for their first space traveler among the jet-fighter pilots of the armed forces. Fighter pilots were accustomed to constant danger, high altitude, high-speed travel, and the need to make crucial decisions in a split second's time. The basic qualifications for a pilot to be considered for Project Mercury were these: The pilot could be no more than 40 years old and no taller than 5 feet, 11 inches (in order to be able to fit into the Mercury capsule). His physical condition had to be excellent. And he had to be a qualified jet pilot with at least 1,500 hours flying time to his credit.

More than 500 pilots met the basic qualifications for Project Mercury. After a review of military and medical records, interviews, and psychological tests, many of the initial 500 were eliminated. The remainder were then subjected to intensive physical and psychological examination at the Lovelace Medical Clinic in Albuquerque, New Mexico, and at the Wright Air Development Center

T. Keith Glennan was the first administrator of the National Aeronautics and Space Administration (NASA), which was founded in July 1958 and absorbed all of the government's many space programs.

in Ohio. Eventually, the group was reduced to just seven. On April 9, 1959, NASA chief T. Keith Glennan held a press conference to introduce the seven ordinary supermen to the world. They were: navy lieutenant M. Scott Carpenter; air force captain L. Gordon Cooper, Jr.; U.S. Marines lieutenant colonel John H. Glenn, Jr.; air force captain Virgil I. ("Gus") Grissom; navy lieutenant commander Walter M. ("Wally") Schirra, Jr.; navy lieutenant commander Alan B. Shepard, Jr.; and air force captain Donald K. ("Deke") Slayton. These seven were prototypical test-pilot types—all-American daredevil aviators who had cut their teeth flying fighter planes in World War II, engaging in high-altitude dogfights with the Chinese in "MiG alley" over Korea during the Korean War, or piloting test flights of the newest, fastest American jet fighters and rocket planes. Within days, the seven were known all across America, and in the next few years they would acquire the status of space-age folk heroes. They were dubbed *astronauts*—star voyagers.

Shortly after the decision to proceed with their own manned spaceflight project, Sergey Korolyov and members of the Soviet Academy of Sciences met to discuss the selection of pilots for Vostok. Like the Americans, they felt that jet-fighter pilots would be best suited for the mission. But the Soviets restricted their consideration to fighter pilots who had experienced some type of in-flight emergency and who had returned to their airfield in the aircraft rather than ejecting. It was felt that this would indicate a pilot's ability to function successfully under conditions of severe stress and danger. Several hundred Soviet pilots had undergone such a crisis without abandoning their vehicle; these pilots were summoned to a military hospital in Moscow for further screening, including a complete medical examination and psychological evaluation. The group was narrowed to 40, then 20, then 6. These six were Yury Gagarin, Anatoly Kartashov, Adrian Nikolayev, Pavel Popovich, Gherman Titov, and Valentin Varlamov. (Kartashov and Varlamov were eventually replaced by Grigary Nelyubov and Valery Bykovsky.) They were dubbed *cosmonauts*—voyagers of the cosmos.

The final intensive training of the cosmonauts and astronauts was fairly similar. The astronauts underwent classroom instruction in such areas as upper-atmosphere physics, aerodynamics, physiology, guidance and navigation, rocket propulsion, communications, meteorology, and astronomy. The cosmonauts attended lectures on space medicine, rocket engines, celestial mechanics, orbital dynamics, and spacecraft design. The astronauts learned star recognition and celestial navigation at the University of North Carolina's Morehead Planetarium. The cosmonauts studied astronomy at the Moscow Planetarium.

A major portion of the astronauts' training was dedicated to egress and survival. Egress training included practicing how to exit the spacecraft underwater in case the capsule flooded or sank after landing on the ocean. (NASA capsules would land, or splash down, on the ocean, whereas the Soviets preferred dry-ground landings.) The astronauts also had to learn jungle, desert, and cold-weather survival tactics, in case an emergency brought them down in a remote area. The cosmonauts also underwent survival training, parachute technique training, and radio communications instruction. Both the cosmonauts and astronauts were subjected to rigorous—and often bewildering—physical and psychological conditioning, and most important, to specialized training that simulated the unique conditions encountered during spaceflight.

Spaceflight conditioning included centrifuge runs (the centrifuge machine is a massive device, not unlike certain carnival rides, consisting of a 50-foot-long circulatory arm

The original seven astronauts pose for a photograph in front of an air force jet in 1959. From left to right are Scott Carpenter, Gordon Cooper, John Glenn, Gus Grissom, Wally Schirra, Alan Shepard, and Deke Slayton.

The Mercury capsule prototype undergoes aerodynamic testing in the full-scale wind tunnel at NASA's Langley Research Center in Hampton, Virginia, January 1959.

that spins a human subject, strapped into a cockpit at the end of the arm, around and around at high speeds and different angles in order to subject the passenger to the kind of intense gravitational forces encountered during spaceflight); heat chamber endurance sessions; decompression chamber sessions; and sensory-deprivation chamber endurance tests. In addition, each cosmonaut had to perform a 3-day simulated flight in a mock-up spacecraft, and the astronauts routinely spent 10-hour sessions in highly detailed Mercury simulators. As spring 1961 approached, engineers for Mercury and Vostok were predicting an April launch. Soon, the final questions would be answered: Which nation would be the first into space? And who among the seven astronauts and six cosmonauts would be the first man in space?

Yury Gagarin was born March 9, 1934, in the village of Klushino, about 100 miles from Moscow. He started school in 1941, but World War II interrupted his formal education. It was a harrowing time for Yury, his family, and for all Russians. Nazi soldiers occupied the Gagarin house during the war, and the family had to live in a dugout. After the war, the Gagarins moved to nearby Gzhatsk, and Yury reentered school. His favorite subjects were mathematics and science. In 1950, he entered a school in Lyubertsy to learn to be a foundryman. A year later, he transferred to a four-year technical school in Saratov, where he would finish his secondary education while studying foundry work. Saratov, on the Volga River, also had a flying school and club, which Gagarin joined while in his final year there. He graduated in 1955 with honors as a foundryman technician, his ground-school diploma from the flying school, and a passion for flying. That summer, he enrolled in an aviation camp, where he learned to fly the Russian Yak-18 aircraft. Gagarin was subsequently accepted as a cadet at the Orenburg Pilot Training School; he graduated two years later as a pilot, first-class.

Gagarin's first posting with the Soviet air force was at Orenburg, where he flew high-performance MiG fighters. In 1959, while serving with a squadron in the Arctic, he applied for admission to the top-secret cosmonaut training group, "if," as he wryly added, "such a group exists." After undergoing the rigorous selection process, Gagarin found himself among the final six cosmonauts. And by noon on April 12, 1961, the entire world had been introduced to the name Yury Gagarin—NASA officials no doubt winced every time they heard it—for on that morning the 27-year-old Russian became the first human being in outer space.

A cosmonaut endures high g forces during a run on a centrifuge machine. The centrifuge machine was integral to the conditioning of both astronauts and cosmonauts, preparing them for the effects of the extreme acceleration experienced during launch and reentry.

"Could One Dream of Anything Greater?"

Early in the morning of April 12, 1961, 27-year-old Red Air Force cosmonaut Yury Gagarin boarded a small bus for the Baikonur Cosmodrome launchpad, located near the remote village of Tyuratam in the Soviet republic of Kazakhstan. Just over two hours remained until the Soviet Union would attempt to launch *Vostok 1* and make Major Gagarin the first man in outer space. If Gagarin was nervous about this momentous—and perilous—journey, he did not show it. Like the other cosmonauts and the astronauts who would follow him into space, Gagarin faced the great unknown that lay before him with equanimity and a sense of humor. During the bus ride to the launch site, he was the one keeping the physicians, technicians, military officers, and fellow cosmonauts who accompanied him from becoming too somber or worried. Just before arriving at the pad, he invited everybody to join him in a song (they declined). Meanwhile, technicians and engineers at the cosmodrome were busy conducting the final crucial checks on the rocket. The little blue-gray bus, now dwarfed by the towering rocket, rolled to a stop as dawn broke over the launch site. Gagarin, clad in a white helmet, black boots, and orange overalls covering his space suit, stepped out and exclaimed, "What a glorious sun!" Then he walked to a microphone near the base of *Vostok 1*, and, with the rocket gleaming behind him in the light of a new dawn, he addressed the small crowd that had gathered there.

Cosmonaut Yury Gagarin, the first human to fly beyond the earth's atmosphere and into outer space. Gagarin, a 27-year-old Red Air Force fighter pilot, made the historic flight aboard Vostok 1 *on April 12, 1961.*

Engineers from Sergey Korolyov's Design Bureau inspect the first Vostok spacecraft as the scheduled launch date draws near. Korolyov's Vostok program beat NASA's Project Mercury into space by less than a month.

"Dear friends," Gagarin began, "you who are close to me, and you whom I do not know, fellow Russians, and people of all countries and continents. In a few minutes a powerful rocket will carry me into the distant realm of space. What can I tell you in these last minutes before launch? My whole life now appears to me as one beautiful moment. All that I previously lived through and did, was lived through and done for the sake of this moment. You can understand that it is difficult for me to analyze my feelings right now, when the critical moment is close at hand, that moment for which we have long—and passionately—been preparing ourselves. I wonder whether it is worthwhile to tell you of the feelings I experienced when I was offered the chance to make this flight? I felt great happiness. To be the first man in space—to meet nature face to face in an unprecedented encounter—could one dream of anything greater? But immediately after that I thought of the tremendous responsibility I bore, to be the first to do what generations of people had dreamed of, to be the first to pave the way into space for mankind. Just tell me if there is any more complex task than the one that has fallen to my lot! This responsibility is not toward one person, not toward a few dozen, not toward a group. It is a responsibility toward all mankind—toward its present and its future."

His speech over, Gagarin boarded the elevator that took him to the top of the launch tower. There, he walked to the platform railing, surveyed the countryside, and waved one last time to the people below. Then technicians helped him into the spacecraft and secured the hatch. Ninety minutes remained until lift-off. These were the most tense moments for the cosmonaut. He was sealed inside the tiny capsule in the rocket's nose, 125 feet above the ground, and despite the steady chatter in his earphones of the engineers conducting the final systems checks, Yury Gagarin was alone with his thoughts and his fears. It was quite possible, the cosmonaut knew, that he might never return to earth alive.

All the preflight checks were complete and *Vostok 1* was ready for launch. Physicians monitoring the cosmonaut's vital signs were pleased to note that he remained calm. When they informed him that everything seemed normal, Gagarin jokingly inquired if his heart was still beating. "Your pulse rate is 64, and your respiration is 24," he was told. "Roger," Gagarin replied, "so my heart is beating." Finally, at 9:07 A.M., the final commands were given: "Hold . . . Ignition . . . Switch to launch . . . Lift-off!" Gagarin heard the whine of the propellant pumps followed by a deep thunderous roar as 32 engines ignited simultaneously, generating 1.1 million pounds' thrust. Those on the ground felt the profound rumble deep in their chest and were momentarily blinded by the burst of flame from the rocket's tail. "We're off!" Gagarin exclaimed. Slowly at first, then faster and faster, the rocket began its climb to the heavens. The world's first manned spaceflight had begun.

Vostok 1 had four booster rockets clustered around a core vehicle. When the boosters exhausted their propellants, about 120 seconds after launch, they were discarded, leaving the vehicle under the power of just the core. The core engines had a combined thrust of 211,000 pounds,

The 125-foot-tall Vostok 1 *launch vehicle prior to blast-off at the Baikonur Cosmodrome. Yury Gagarin, enclosed within a tiny capsule attached to the nose of the rocket, would be propelled into space as the rocket generated more than 1 million pounds' thrust.*

and *Vostok 1* continued to gain altitude. The tremendous rate at which the rocket gained speed increased the force of gravity on the cosmonaut; acceleration reached a peak of five g's, which meant that Gagarin felt as though he were five times heavier than his normal weight. (The term

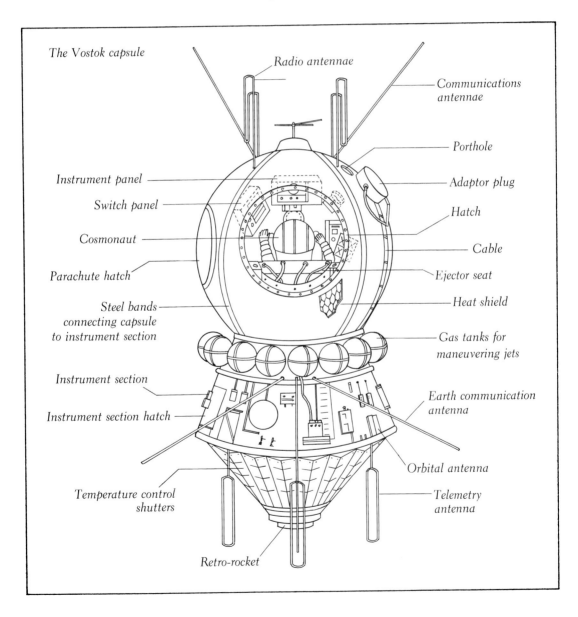

The Vostok capsule

Radio antennae

Communications antennae

Porthole

Instrument panel

Switch panel

Cosmonaut

Parachute hatch

Steel bands connecting capsule to instrument section

Instrument section

Instrument section hatch

Temperature control shutters

Retro-rocket

Adaptor plug

Hatch

Cable

Ejector seat

Heat shield

Gas tanks for maneuvering jets

Earth communication antenna

Orbital antenna

Telemetry antenna

Gaining altitude, Vostok 1 would shed its various boosters as they exhausted their fuel, until only this capsule remained. Gagarin, sealed within the capsule, would experience high g forces from the intense acceleration of the boosters and then weightlessness as the boosters fell away and orbit was established.

g represents a unit of force equal to the force exerted by gravity on a body at rest and is used to indicate the force to which a body is subjected when accelerated. A person standing on the earth's surface is subjected to one g and experiences his or her normal weight.) Despite the crushing pressure on his body, Gagarin continued talking to mission control, reporting that he felt fine.

After *Vostok 1* passed through the lower atmosphere, the nose shroud that covered the capsule separated. Gagarin could then see out the three portholes and observe the sky turning from dark blue to black as he left the atmosphere behind. About 300 seconds after lift-off, the core exhausted its fuel and was jettisoned. The upper stage, attached directly to the spacecraft, ignited and finished the task of propelling Vostok 1 away from the earth and into orbit. The g forces eased off and soon Gagarin was weightless; only his straps prevented the cosmonaut from floating freely about the cabin. Fourteen minutes after launch the upper stage was jettisoned, and Gagarin reported, "Separation from the carrier rocket completed." Vostok 1 was now in orbit around the earth. It was an elliptical orbit, with an apogee, or high point in relation to the earth, of 204 miles, and a perigee, or the point where it passed closest to the earth, of 113 miles.

Gazing down at the earth below—a phenomenal sight— Gagarin reported that he felt alright and was experiencing no ill effects from weightlessness. He sampled food from a squeeze tube and drank some water. Although his flight was only scheduled to last one orbit and food was not necessary, scientists on the ground wanted to make sure that weightlessness did not interfere with a person's ability to eat. Passing into the darkness of the earth's shadow, Gagarin marveled at the view. At 9:51 A.M., Vostok 1 emerged from the earth's shadow and was once again bathed in brilliant sunlight. Because there was no atmosphere for it to be filtered through, the sunlight was dazzling in its purity. As the spacecraft emerged into the light, a sensor in its optical system automatically locked onto the sun and sent signals to the maneuvering jets, which fired and placed Vostok 1 in the proper attitude. (Attitude, used in a spaceflight context, is the position of the craft in reference to a fixed point such as the earth. According to astronaut Michael Collins, "Attitude really means which way something is pointed. Up, down, toward the sun, or what?")

At the time of Vostok 1, the effects of sustained weightlessness were still unknown, and there were those within

The Vostok 1 *cosmonaut couch was especially contoured to cushion the pilot against the rigors of launch, reentry, and ejection. After reentry and descent, the couch and cosmonaut would be ejected from the capsule. A parachute would be deployed, the couch would fall away, and the cosmonaut would float safely back to earth.*

the Soviet Academy of Sciences who feared a cosmonaut might become incapacitated and unable to control his craft. Therefore, on this first flight, the manual controls had been disengaged; *Vostok 1* was being piloted by automatic onboard systems and ground control. Gagarin was only a passenger. (Like his American counterparts, Gagarin abhorred this state of affairs.) But just in case something went wrong with the control link to the ground or with the craft's onboard systems, Gagarin had a means of taking manual control. A three-digit code that would activate the manual override system was inside a sealed envelope in the cabin. All systems worked perfectly, however, and—to his own disappointment—Gagarin never had to open the envelope.

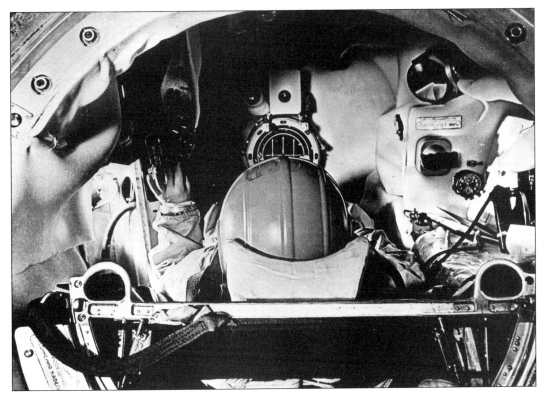

Passing over the vast blue curvature of the Atlantic, Gagarin thought of his mother and wondered how she would react to the news of his flight through space. In the small Russian village of Gzhatsk (later to be renamed Gagarin in honor of the cosmonaut), Anna Gagarin heard the news over the radio at about 10:00 A.M.. Up until that moment, she had been unaware that Yury was involved in space exploration. Overwhelmed at the thought that her son was now circling the earth like a human *Sputnik*, she rushed to the train station and boarded a train for Moscow to be with her daughter-in-law Valya and her two small granddaughters. (Valya Gagarin had been told of her husband's activities but not of the actual launch date.) The cosmonaut's father learned the astounding news that Yury was in orbit around the earth after he returned home from work that morning.

Cosmonaut Gagarin, viewed from above, snug within the Vostok 1 capsule. Unlike the sophisticated and highly sensitive jet fighters he was used to flying, Gagarin could exert only limited control over the first Vostok spacecraft.

Yury Gagarin, in the meantime, was passing over the continent of Africa, and he was certainly more calm and collected than his parents or his wife. At 10:15 A.M., the automatic pilot turned *Vostok 1* around, maneuvering it into the proper position for firing the retro-rocket, which would, it was hoped, break the momentum of the orbit and thus allow the craft to succumb to the gravitational pull of the earth. This was a particularly nerve-racking moment for the cosmonaut and everyone else in mission control. Two of the five test flights that had preceded *Vostok 1* had ended in failure at this point. This time, the retro-rocket worked perfectly and slowed the spacecraft by nearly 350 miles per hour, enough so it could drop from orbit and reenter the atmosphere.

For the cosmonaut, reentry was harrowing. Immediately following retrofire, with the spacecraft still 3,700 miles from touchdown, explosive bolts released the capsule

Vostok 1 rests in the field where it landed after its historic flight into space. The primitive-looking sphere functioned perfectly, carrying Yury Gagarin around the earth once before returning him safely to Soviet soil.

from the equipment section, which was no longer needed. All that remained of the 125-foot giant launched just over an hour before was the 7½-foot-diameter capsule and the man within, now plummeting earthward at better than 17,000 miles per hour. When the capsule first reached the atmosphere, it began oscillating, and Gagarin became unnerved for the first time. The oscillations soon stopped, however, because of the capsule's aerodynamic design (at mission control, this was noted by Korolyov with satisfaction). Now the g loading on Gagarin reached a peak of 10 g's, and the Russian felt like a 1,500-pound brick falling from the sky. Looking out the windows, he could see streaks of fire. The friction generated by reentry into the atmosphere caused the capsule to heat up like a meteor. To protect the occupant, the capsule's exterior had been covered with an ablative material—a substance that would burn away and vaporize, taking much of the heat with it.

Despite the fire and the 2,000 degree Fahrenheit temperature outside, the temperature inside the cabin remained a constant 68 degrees Fahrenheit.

Now, Gagarin saw the blackness of space outside the portholes give way to blue sky. He braced himself for ejection. Ejection was necessary because the capsule's descent speed was too high to allow a survivable landing for the cosmonaut. (With a personal parachute, a cosmonaut would land with a speed of 16 feet per second; the capsule, with its parachute, would land at nearly twice that.) Looking out the portholes a final time, Gagarin could see the welcome sights of the Volga River and the town of Saratov rushing up at him. The capsule's parachute deployed, slowing its fall to about 450 miles per hour. At 26,000

Yury Gagarin's face reflects the cosmonaut's exhilaration in a photograph taken an hour after his return to earth following the flight of Vostok 1.

feet, the capsule's hatch blew off and two rockets catapulted the cosmonaut and his seat out and away. Gagarin's own parachute deployed a few seconds later, with the cosmonaut still in the ejection seat. At 13,000 feet, the seat fell away. Gagarin, floating to earth beneath an orange-and-white parachute, noted with satisfaction that he would land near Saratov. The town had a special, personal significance to Gagarin, for it was near there that he had taken his first flight in an airplane. He would later comment, "It all happened as in a good novel. I returned from space in the same place where I had first flown a plane." The cosmonaut floated gently down from the sky and came to rest in the plowed field of a collective farm. The capsule landed not far away.

The NASA Mercury-Redstone 3 booster and capsule at Cape Canaveral, Florida. Next to the rocket is the gantry (launch tower) and cherry picker, used by the astronauts to enter the capsule atop the rocket.

For cosmonaut Gagarin and the Soviet Union, the flight of *Vostok 1* provided the satisfaction of "a good novel," as Gagarin put it, but in the United States, the news that the rival superpower had put a man in space was greeted with dismay—it was clear that the Soviets were well ahead of the Americans in the space race. NASA officials had hoped that the Mercury-Redstone 3 (Mercury was the type of capsule, Redstone the type of booster rocket, and there had been two previous unmanned Mercury-Redstone flights) would carry the first human beyond the atmosphere, and there was deep disappointment throughout NASA when word of Gagarin's flight came through. Despite the disappointment, preparations for the Mercury-Redstone 3 mission continued. It was imperative that a U.S. astronaut follow the Russian cosmonaut into space as soon as possible.

The announcement was made on May 2: America's first man in space was to be navy lieutenant commander Alan B. Shepard, Jr. Shepard was born on November 18, 1923, in tiny East Derry, New Hampshire. His father was a career military man, an army colonel, and there was never any doubt in the family that Al would also join the service. After graduating from the United States Naval Academy in 1944, he served aboard the destroyer USS *Cogswell* in the Pacific during World War II. Shepard later entered flight training at Corpus Christi, Texas, and got his wings in 1947. Three years later, after several tours aboard aircraft carriers in the Mediterranean Sea, he attended the United States Navy Test Pilot School at Patuxent River, Maryland. He soon acquired a reputation as one of the navy's premier test pilots, breaking in new, highly volatile jet fighters such as the F11F Tigercat and the F2H3 Banshee. Tough, cool, and unflappable, Shepard volunteered for Project Mercury and survived the rigorous screening process to become one of the final seven original astronauts, and then *the* astronaut, the man who would ride the Mercury-Redstone 3.

The seven Project Mercury astronauts pose for a photograph in their space suits. Alan B. Shepard (back row, left) would be the first American in outer space. He would be followed into space, chronologically, by Gus Grissom (back row, center); John Glenn (front row, third from the left); Scott Carpenter (front row, extreme right); Wally Schirra (front row, extreme left); and Gordon Cooper (back row, right). Donald Slayton (front row, second from left) was grounded because of a heart murmur.

Astronaut Alan Shepard is sealed into the Freedom 7 *capsule prior to lift-off. If a crisis developed on the launchpad, Shepard would not be able to exit the capsule until it had been blasted away from the booster by a small emergency rocket and brought back to the ground via a parachute.*

Shepard named his capsule *Freedom 7*, the "7" standing for the original seven astronauts. Mercury engineers had chosen the army's powerful Redstone missile to carry the capsule into space. McDonnell Aircraft of St. Louis built the Mercury capsule. It was bell shaped, with a conical portion containing the cabin topped by a short cylinder housing the recovery parachutes. It was 132 inches long, 74.5 inches in diameter, and weighed about 4,000 pounds. An ablative heat shield covered its base. Three retro-rockets were mounted in a washtub-shaped package strapped to the heat shield. The Mercury capsule could not *translate*, or alter its orbit, but, like the Vostok capsule, it could change its attitude using hydrogen peroxide thrusters. (*Translation*, according to astronaut Collins, "means *moving* through space, be it up or down, left or right.")

The cabin atmosphere was pure oxygen, maintained at a pressure of 5.1 pounds per square inch. This represents slightly more than the oxygen content of the earth's atmosphere at sea level. To enable him to endure the acceleration encountered during launch and reentry, the astronaut sat in a fiberglass couch molded to fit his body. An orange tower topped with a rocket motor was attached to the capsule's nose during launch. This was the launch escape system. If the booster malfunctioned, or if there was an emergency on the pad, the rocket motor would pull the capsule and its human occupant away from the volatile Redstone, after which a parachute would deploy and gently bring the capsule to earth.

The final countdown began at 8:30 P.M. on May 4, for a 7:00 A.M. lift-off from Cape Canaveral, Florida. Shepard was awakened at 1:10 A.M. to begin preparing for the flight. After a shower, he ate a breakfast of orange juice, filet mignon, and scrambled eggs with his backup pilot John Glenn, physician William K. Douglas, and a few other launch team members. At 2:40 A.M., he was given a physical examination and pronounced fit for the mission. Shepard then put on his shiny silver space suit. The Project Mercury space suit was built by the B. F. Goodrich Company for NASA. It comprised two layers: a neoprene (synthetic rubber)-impregnated nylon pressure bladder covered by an aluminized nylon outer layer. Beneath the suit, the astronaut wore underwear with built-in ventilation panels.

By 3:55 A.M., Shepard was fully suited and had left the astronaut quarters for the transfer van and the trip to Cape Canaveral Pad 5. At 5:15 A.M., Shepard stepped out of the van and into the glare of the brilliant launchpad lights, walked over to the gantry, and boarded the elevator. Five minutes later, he climbed into *Freedom 7*. The astronaut quickly established contact with mission control and began reading off the prelaunch checklist. At T-minus 15 minutes (15 minutes before launch), clouds moved in. Meteorologists predicted that the sky would clear within 40 minutes, so a "hold" was called. A few minutes later, another hold was called to replace a power inverter in the

(continued on page 52)

Mach 1 and Beyond

While Alan Shepard and the other Mercury astronauts were flying into space aboard Redstone- and Atlas-powered spacecraft, rocket vehicles of a different kind were being flown regularly over Edwards Air Force Base (formerly Muroc Army Air Field) in southern California's Antelope Valley. And although the "original seven" astronauts were, at that time, the only astronauts known to the public and recognized as such, the test pilots flying the experimental X-15 rocket planes in the desert skies over Muroc Dry Lake were becoming astronauts in their own right. Like the Mercury astronauts, the test pilots at Edwards were flying vehicles beyond the 50-mile limit of the earth's atmosphere; the test pilots, however, were doing something that the Mercury astronauts could not do—returning to the runway and landing their vehicles like traditional airplanes.

The goal of the first of the X series (X stands for experimental) aircraft, the Bell X-1, built by the Bell Aircraft Corporation under an army contract in 1946, was to break Mach 1, the speed of sound, which is about 700 miles per hour, although it can vary by as much as 100 miles per hour depending on altitude and atmospheric conditions. Pilots who had approached Mach 1 before the appearance of the X-1 in 1947 reported violent buffeting and other hazardous aerodynamic occurrences; some planes went spinning out of control or even disintegrated when they reached this sonic barrier. Many pilots and engineers felt it would be impossible to break the speed of sound. World War II fighter-pilot ace Chuck Yeager of West Virginia, working as a test pilot at Muroc, disagreed; he felt that the buffeting and violent aerodynamic effects would ease off just before Mach 1 was reached. Yeager was right. On October 14, 1947, he flew the X-1 through the sound barrier—there was a tremendous boom over the desert as the barrier was broken—and reached Mach 1.05.

In the spring of 1958, the X-15 was unveiled. Developed by NACA in conjunction with the army and navy, and built by North American Aviation, the X-15 was a rocket-powered, stubby winged, streamlined, 50-foot-long monster. A select group of test pilots was assigned to the extremely dangerous X-

15 program. The initial group comprised air force captains Ivan Kincheloe and Robert White; navy commander Forrest Peterson; NACA pilots Joseph Walker, Neil Armstrong, and John McKay; and A. Scott Crossfield and Alvin White of North American. The X-15's builders believed that the craft could fly at speeds beyond Mach 6 and at altitudes above 50 miles. It would be the test pilots' job to push the X-15 to its limits. Some of the aviators would get killed in the process; others would have the profound experience of

blasting the aircraft up through the thinning atmosphere into the darkness above, where the sun, the stars, and the moon were all out at once, and then guiding it back down to earth for a landing on a desert runway.

On November 9, 1961, test pilot Robert White set an airspeed record of mach 6.04 in an X-15. On the 62nd flight of the program, White flew his X-15 to an altitude of 314,750 feet—over 59 miles. Fifty miles was recognized as the boundary where the earth's atmosphere gives way to outer space, so this flight, made more than three months before John Glenn's Mercury-Atlas 6 mission, qualified White as an astronaut. He was the first person to achieve astronaut status while flying a winged aircraft. Six other pilots would also achieve astronaut status flying the X-15.

An engineer at Langley Research Center, Hampton, Virginia, makes an adjustment on a model of the X-15 rocket plane before aerodynamic testing in a wind tunnel begins. The X-15's streamlined shape was designed to reduce transonic drag effects, which reduce velocity.

(continued from page 49)

Redstone. After the count was resumed, a problem was found in a computer at the Goddard Space Flight Center in Greenbelt, Maryland, which caused another delay (a nationwide computer network facilitated the launch and flight). Finally, after a total hold time of 2 hours and 34 minutes, the countdown progressed with no further difficulties. All across the country, the routine activities of day-to-day life came to a halt as Americans, glued to their radios and televisions, waited for the launch.

"LOX [liquid oxygen] tank pressurized . . . Vehicle power . . . Thirty seconds." Finally, at 9:34 A.M.: "Ignition . . . Mainstage . . . Lift-off!" "Roger," Shepard responded from inside *Freedom 7*, "lift-off, and the clock is started." As the Redstone accelerated into the sky, Shepard experienced g-loading of up to 6.2 g's. The astronaut reported "booster cutoff" 142 seconds after launch; the Redstone had done its job, and *Freedom 7* was traveling at 5,180 miles per hour. Ten seconds later, explosive bolts on the clamp that held the capsule to the Redstone detonated, releasing the spacecraft from its carrier. Clear of the Redstone, *Freedom 7*'s automatic control system turned the spacecraft around so that it flew heat shield first. "What a beautiful view!" America's first man in space exclaimed.

Four minutes and 44 seconds into the flight, *Freedom 7* achieved its apogee of 116.5 miles and the retrofire sequence began. Thirty seconds later, with the capsule in the proper attitude for reentry, the three retro-rockets fired in sequence. As the spacecraft slammed downward through the atmosphere, Shepard endured 11 g's. Then the pressure disappeared and the parachutes deployed. First was the 6-foot-diameter drogue parachute, released at an altitude of 21,000 feet to stabilize the capsule. Then, at 10,000 feet, the 63-foot-diameter main parachute deployed. (In case anything went wrong with the main parachute, the capsule carried an identical reserve parachute.) Shepard splashed down in the Atlantic within sight of the recovery helicopters and 302 miles from the Cape Canaveral launch site. His flight had lasted 15 minutes, 22 seconds. After being retrieved by the helicopters, the astronaut and *Freedom 7* were taken to the aircraft carrier USS *Lake Champlain.*

Compared to Yury Gagarin's orbital flight, Shepard's brief 15-minute up-and-down jaunt was a mere stroll in the park. Shepard himself seemed hardly overwhelmed by the journey—he described it as "just a pleasant flight." But the propaganda yield was enormous; Shepard and the other six astronauts became instant national heroes and received adulation from the public and the media that was reminiscent of the wild acclaim heaped upon aviator Charles Lindbergh following his transatlantic flight. In terms of the politics of their times, Gagarin had scored a great victory for the Soviet Union and the ideology it represented, and Shepard had served notice for the United States that the Soviets would be challenged every step of the way. Cold war politics aside, however, a much more significant victory had been won, for on April 12, 1961, cosmonaut Yury Gagarin had broken through the confines of the earth's atmosphere once and for all.

After splashdown, a U.S. Marine helicopter team lifts Alan Shepard away from the Freedom 7 *capsule, which floats below him on the surface of the Atlantic. Shepard's suborbital flight lasted 15 minutes, covered 302 miles, and marked a successful beginning to NASA's Project Mercury.*

"Dawn of a New Age"

The two rival space programs now began a kind of duel in outer space, with Chief Designer Korolyov and the new NASA administrator, James E. Webb, each spurred on by his own government, engaged in an ongoing contest of orbital one-upmanship. At times, the politics threatened to obscure the true significance of the flights, but several harrowing incidents and near disasters reminded everyone involved that although the tools had become more sophisticated, the nature of exploration remained basically the same—a human pitted against an unknown and hostile new environment.

Ten weeks after Shepard's flight, another Mercury-Redstone blasted off from the pad at Cape Canaveral. Named *Liberty Bell 7*, the spacecraft carried Captain Virgil I. ("Gus") Grissom, a 35-year-old air force test pilot from Indiana who had flown over 100 combat missions in F-86 Sabre jets during the Korean War. Grissom's flight plan differed from Shepard's; at the insistence of the astronauts, the little portholes used to see out of *Freedom 7* had been replaced by a larger rectangular window, and Grissom was to spend more time on outside observations.

Grissom's suborbital flight went according to plan for the most part. *Liberty Bell 7* achieved an apogee of 118.3 miles, while the astronaut tested the spacecraft's manual controls and marveled at the view from the new window.

NASA astronaut Gus Grissom suits up for his Mercury-Redstone 4 mission on July 21, 1961. Grissom's 15-minute suborbital flight proceeded much like Alan Shepard's Mercury-Redstone 3 mission until splashdown, when Grissom's capsule, Liberty Bell 7, lost its hatch prematurely, took on water, and sank.

Retrofire, reentry, and descent were normal and Grissom splashed down on the Atlantic within two miles of the recovery ship. It was here, on the ocean, rather than in outer space, that the problems began. Grissom had gone through the postlanding checklist, unbuckled his restraints, and was preparing to blow the hatch when he heard a "muffled thud." The hatch cover had blown away prematurely and seawater was pouring into the capsule! While recovery helicopters hovered above, both the capsule and Grissom's space suit filled with water; *Liberty Bell 7* sank to the bottom of the Atlantic, and Grissom himself almost sank with it. The loss of the capsule was a disaster for NASA engineers and scientists, and the near loss of Gus Grissom reminded everyone of the ever-present dangers faced by the astronauts. Grissom himself was annoyed but undaunted, and he was ready and willing to fly again, which he would do for the Gemini program. His luck would not change for the better, however, and his career as an astronaut would prove to be particularly ill fated.

While NASA officials were attempting to figure out what went wrong with Grissom's hatch—"I didn't do anything, the damned thing just blew" was Grissom's only explanation—Korolyov was making the final preparations for the Soviet space program's next ambitious step. *Vostok 2* would make a 24-hour orbital flight. Yury Gagarin's backup pilot, Gherman Titov, a 26-year-old graduate of the Volgograd Air Force Pilots School, would man the second Vostok.

Titov blasted off aboard *Vostok 2* on August 6, 1961. During the initial orbit, Titov activated the Vostok manual control system for the first time. On the third orbit, he ate his first meal in space—unappetizing soup, meat, and liver pastes from squeeze tubes. About seven hours after launch, during the fifth orbit, Titov became nauseated and disoriented. These discomforts were particularly acute when he turned his head sharply to follow the motion of

(continued on page 65)

Things to Come

One stage of the appropriately named Titan booster that would power the Gemini craft and its passengers into space.

The advent of the age of space exploration added new concepts and new images to American popular culture, and new words and phrases to the American lexicon. Terms such as *booster rocket*, *lift-off*, *orbit*, *splashdown*, *space suit*, and *space walk*, which at first seemed to represent an intimidating new technology, soon became a comfortable part of the daily vocabulary of America's adults and schoolchildren. The images behind the words were quickly assimilated as well. Awe inspiring and beautiful—gigantic silver rockets ascending into the heavens on tongues of fire, tiny capsules passing silently through a vast darkness, humans in pressurized suits clinging to the outside of hurtling spacecraft, planet earth as seen from outer space—they captured the eye of the photographer as well as the imagination of the public. That the idea of space travel has lost some of the excitement and mystery that surrounded it during the first, heady years of Mercury and Gemini is reflected in current usage: Astronauts no longer fly rocket ships, they fly *space shuttles*. (NASA could hardly have come up with a more mundane term for this remarkable craft.) One way to recapture the sense of wonder felt during those early years is through photographs. No other human endeavor has presented the camera's eye with such striking and magnificent sights. Even now, on the cusp of the millennium, these photographs are captivating and stimulating, for although they reflect images of the past, they also speak of things to come.

Multiple exposures provide a visual chronicle of the erection of the Gemini-Titan spaceship on the launchpad at Cape Kennedy, Florida, in 1966.

The Atlas booster, with the Mercury capsule poised at its peak, waits next to the launch tower at Cape Canaveral.

Lift-off: Battling gravity, the Gemini-Titan III spaceship climbs slowly away from the launch tower during the first, agonizing seconds following ignition.

An Aerobee, one of the rockets used during the early days of the American space program, blasts off from White Sands Proving Ground in New Mexico. Early staging is occurring; the Aerobee can be seen separating from its booster.

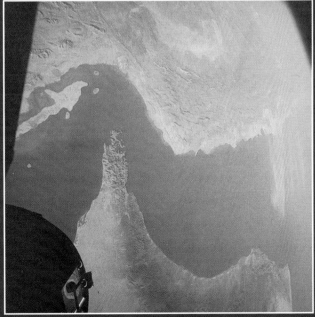

The Persian Gulf area as seen by Gemini-Titan XII astronauts Buzz Aldrin and James Lovell. The Persian Gulf, on the left, narrows into the Strait of Hormuz, which flows into the Gulf of Oman at the right. The land mass at the top is Iran; at the bottom is the United Arab Emirates.

Celestial body: Free of the earth's gravity, but not of its beauty, Ed White soars along with Gemini 4.

Rendezvous in space: Gemini 8 docks with the Agena target vehicle, and two spacecraft become one. This photograph was taken by astronaut David Scott from the copilot's seat of the Gemini.

Spacewalker: Gemini-Titan IV astronaut Edward H. White II unravels the tether connecting him to the spacecraft during the first moments of his June 3, 1965, extravehicular excursion.

The new frontier: A time-lapse photograph of the Milky Way galaxy as seen from the earth's location on the outer edge of one of the galaxy's spiral arms. (The bright, straight line is the trail of a passing satellite.)

Mercury-Redstone 4 blasts off from Cape Canaveral. The main portion of the vehicle is the Redstone booster rocket. The Mercury capsule, with Gus Grissom inside, sits atop the Redstone, which will fall away in sections as the ascent progresses, leaving only the capsule to return to earth.

(continued from page 56)
weightless objects floating about in the cabin. What Titov experienced is today referred to as Space Adaptation Syndrome. This problem is still not fully understood, and there appears to be no way to predict who will be susceptible. About one-third of all people engaged in spaceflight

will suffer from Space Adaptation Syndrome, although the symptoms usually disappear after two or three days. In 1961, such facts were still unknown, and Titov's symptoms caused some alarm among Soviet physicians monitoring his flight. On his seventh orbit, ground controllers instructed him to try to sleep, hoping the rest would help him feel better. (The Soviet doctors need not have worried; it would take more than an upset stomach to stop Titov. After the flight, he revealed that he had broken his wrist

Gus Grissom, his space suit full of water, is hauled from the Atlantic after his disastrous splashdown on the morning of July 21, 1961. The Liberty Bell 7 *has just begun its journey to the bottom of the ocean.*

in a childhood bicycle accident; the injury had never been treated and had not healed correctly. After becoming an aviation cadet, Titov feared that the old injury would ruin his chances of becoming a pilot, so he did not report it but got up early every morning to strengthen the wrist with exercise on the parallel bars. He managed to keep the injury secret, even throughout the cosmonaut screening process. After the flight, physicians stated that had the injury been detected beforehand, Titov would not have been allowed to fly in space.) Titov's condition improved slightly after sleeping, and he finished his flight much as Gagarin did, with an ejection from the reentry capsule. And like Gagarin, Titov received the title Hero of the Soviet Union and the Order of Lenin.

Had there been such a title as Hero of the United States, it most certainly would have been bestowed upon astronaut John Glenn, whose Mercury-Atlas 6 flight, more than any other—including Neil Armstrong's Apollo 11 moon flight in 1969—captured the imagination of the American public. By early 1962, James Webb was ready to duplicate the Soviet chief designer's feat of putting a man in orbit around the earth. A rocket more powerful than the Redstone was required for this, and after numerous—and frequently disastrous—tests, the Atlas rocket was pronounced ready.

Lieutenant Colonel John H. Glenn, Jr., was selected to be the first American to orbit the earth. He was born on July 18, 1921, in Cambridge, Ohio. Glenn joined the Marine Corps in 1943, in time to fly 59 combat missions in the Pacific theater during World War II. In the Korean War, he flew 90 combat missions; in the last 9 days of the conflict, during confrontations in the aerial combat zone over the Yalu River, Glenn downed 3 Soviet-designed MiG fighters. After Korea, he attended the navy's test pilot school at Patuxent River. Even before his orbital flight, Glenn was the most popular of the original seven astronauts. His boyish good looks and a disarmingly sincere and outspoken patriotism endeared him to the American press and public, and the flight itself eclipsed the accomplishments of all his fellow astronauts.

By February 20, 1962, the mammoth Atlas rocket and the worldwide network of recovery teams and tracking stations—the recovery force comprised 24 ships, more than 60 aircraft, and 10,000 people—were ready for launch, and Glenn, after a hearty preflight breakfast of steak, scrambled eggs, toast, orange juice, and coffee, was ready also. Glenn later recalled the blast-off of *Friendship 7*: "When the countdown reached zero, I could feel the engines start. The spacecraft shook, not violently but very solidly. There was no doubt when lift-off occurred." The Atlas powered the spacecraft into an elliptical orbit with an apogee of 163 miles and a perigee of 100 miles. As Glenn streaked over Africa at 17,543 miles per hour, he told the tracking station on the Canary Islands that he could see "dust storms down there blowing across the desert, a lot of dust; it's difficult to see the ground in some areas."

Over the Indian Ocean, he saw his first orbital sunset, the first of three he would see during the flight. "The sunset was beautiful," he reported. "It went down very rapidly. I still have a brilliant blue band clear across the horizon almost covering my whole window. The redness of the sunset I can still see through some of the clouds way over to the left of my course." Glenn and *Friendship 7* passed into the night. Sailing over western Australia, he saw a bright glowing spot on the earth's surface. This was the city of Perth. Although it was around midnight in Australia, the entire population of Perth had stayed awake and turned on every light in the city to send a hello to the solitary American passing above them through the huge, lonely darkness of outer space. For the astronaut, it was a welcome sight.

Trouble began near the end of the first orbit; one of the capsule's thrusters malfunctioned and Glenn had to assume manual control. A touchy situation developed: If the manual attitude control used too much fuel to keep the capsule stable during the orbits, there might not be enough fuel left to position the spacecraft for a correct reentry into the atmosphere. If the capsule came in at too shallow an angle, it would skip off the atmosphere like a flat stone on a calm lake and end up in what would be for the astronaut a permanent orbit—one that would last far longer than the spacecraft's oxygen supply. If, on the other hand, the capsule came in at too steep an angle, it, and the astronaut within, would become something like a shooting star, burning to a cinder as they passed through the atmosphere.

These thoughts were on John Glenn's mind as he completed a second orbit and began a third. During the third orbit, as he cruised backward over Hawaii and watched electrical storms flash and flicker beneath a storm front, mission control gave him some more bad news: Their instruments indicated that the capsule's heat shield was loose. If this were true, *Friendship 7* would be incinerated

Yury Gagarin (left) consults with fellow cosmonaut Gherman Titov, who was to fly Vostok 2. *Gagarin played a major part in the training of the cosmonauts who followed him into space.*

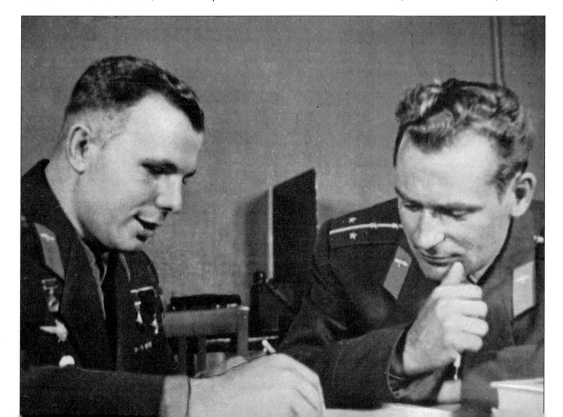

The second cosmonaut to go into space, Major Gherman Titov, and his backup, Adrian Nikolayev, on their way to the Baikonur Cosmodrome on August 6, 1961. Titov orbited the earth 17 times in 25 hours on August 6 and 7, 1961, proving that the Soviet program was well ahead of NASA.

during reentry no matter what angle it assumed. Fearing the worst, Glenn fired the retro-rockets. Using the automatic controls that still worked as well as the manual hand controls to hold the correct attitude, he braced himself for reentry.

As he slammed into the atmosphere, Glenn lost all radio contact with NASA. The capsule was buffeted violently as it plummeted toward the earth, and he struggled to keep it steady with the hand controls. The g forces were tremendous, crushing his chest. There was a hissing noise from outside the capsule and Glenn saw fire and chunks of flaming matter flying past the window; he thought it must be the loose heat shield breaking apart and burning. Glenn expected to burn up in a similar fashion at any second. And then suddenly he was through; there were blue skies outside the windows and *Friendship* 7 was floating gently, under its parachutes, down to the ocean. Glenn, sweating profusely, heard mission control over the radio again. "How are you doing?" a nervous voice inquired. "Oh, pretty good," Glenn replied calmly. Then splash! He was down.

NASA soon learned that the loose heat-shield signal had been wrong; the burning fragments had come from the retro package and the heat shield had remained intact. Nevertheless, the public and the media—to the dismay of Alan Shepard and Gus Grissom—hailed Glenn as America's first space-age hero. While Glenn was cruising down New York City's Broadway in the back of an open convertible enjoying a massive ticker tape parade in his honor, NASA was readying the next spaceflight, eager to take advantage of the momentum generated by Glenn. Air force captain Donald K. ("Deke") Slayton was originally scheduled to pilot Mercury-Atlas 7, until NASA physicians discovered that he had a heart murmur and replaced him with 37-year-old M. Scott Carpenter. (Slayton was bitterly disappointed. Insisting that there was nothing wrong with his heart, he began a 13-year campaign to get himself reinstated as an active astronaut; he finally made it into outer space in the 1975 Apollo-Soyuz Test Program.)

Lieutenant Malcolm Scott Carpenter, of Boulder, Colorado, was another graduate of the navy test pilot school. He dubbed the Mercury-Atlas 7 spacecraft *Aurora* 7 because, in his own words, "I think of Project Mercury and the open manner in which we are conducting it for the benefit of all as a light in the sky. Aurora also means dawn—in this case the dawn of a new age."

Aurora 7 completed three earth orbits on May 24, 1962, while Carpenter engaged in a number of experiments for NASA scientists. *Friendship 7* had proved that man could survive in orbit; *Aurora 7* was to show that an astronaut could work in space. Everything went fairly well until reentry. Carpenter fired the retro-rockets 3 seconds late and the capsule's angle during reentry was off about 25 degrees to the right; subsequently, *Aurora 7* splashed down 250 miles from the planned recovery point—ample evidence of the huge consequences that could result from the most minute errors or miscalculations during spaceflight. After 40 tense minutes during which Carpenter's status was unknown—"I'm afraid we may have lost an astronaut," Walter Cronkite intoned grimly over national television—the astronaut was located, floating contentedly alongside *Aurora 7* in his life raft and passing the time by observing some seaweed and "a black fish." A helicopter picked up the intrepid Carpenter and deposited him, appropriately, on the deck of the aircraft carrier USS *Intrepid*. The entire nation breathed a sigh of relief.

A year had gone by since the last Soviet spaceflight, but the chief designer had not been idle—he had prepared a grand surprise for NASA officials who thought they were beginning to catch up with the Soviet program. *Vostok 3* began its flight much like the previous Vostoks, blasting off from Baikonur on August 11, 1962. The cosmonaut was 33-year-old Red Air Force pilot Adrian ("Iron Man") Nikolayev. (His fellow cosmonauts called him Iron Man because of the durability and resiliency he displayed during spaceflight training.) NASA people were sure that *Vostok 3* would be a long duration flight and they were correct; by August 12, Nikolayev had completed 16 orbits and become the first cosmonaut or astronaut to float freely in the cabin. The surprise came as *Vostok 3* passed over Baikonur Cosmodrome on its 16th orbit. At that moment,

Vostok 4 was launched from the same pad *Vostok 3* had taken off from. Launch occurred within a second of the desired time, and the booster performance was perfect, so *Vostok 4*, piloted by Pavel Popovich, a carpenter turned cosmonaut, assumed an orbit that was almost identical to *Vostok 3*'s.

Astronaut John Glenn is prepared for a centrifuge run during training for the Mercury-Atlas 6 mission. Physicians in the centrifuge chamber will monitor Glenn's vital signs during the run in order to gauge the astronaut's physiological responses to extreme acceleration.

Nikolayev and Popovich flew to within four miles of one another, and visual contact was established. The two cosmonauts communicated throughout the mission, and maintained simultaneous schedules, eating, working, and sleeping at the same time. Both spacecraft contained television cameras, and audiences throughout the Soviet Union and Europe watched the cosmonauts demonstrate the effects of weightlessness. On August 15, after completing 64 orbits in 96 hours, Nikolayev touched down in the Soviet Union. Seven minutes later, Popovich, who had orbited 48 times, landed 125 miles away.

The joint mission was a stunning and unprecedented success for the Soviet Union. NASA officials were appalled, as was the U.S. government; the ability to launch a pair of manned spacecraft from the same launchpad only a day apart, and the ability to direct two missions simultaneously, was undeniable proof of the superiority of the Soviet space program.

With the cold war at its peak—October 1962's Cuban missile crisis saw the world brought to the brink of nuclear war—President John F. Kennedy was putting pressure on NASA to complete Project Mercury and begin Project Gemini, which he hoped would close the "space gap" that existed between the U.S. and Soviet space programs. On October 3, 1962, up went Mercury-Atlas 8, piloted by Lieutenant Commander Wally Schirra of Hackensack, New Jersey, another veteran of the Korean War dogfights and a test pilot for the navy. *Sigma 7* completed 6 orbits during what Schirra described as a "text-book" flight lasting 9 hours and 13 minutes. Mercury-Atlas 9, the final flight of the Mercury series, was piloted by Captain L. Gordon Cooper of the air force, who set a new standard for extreme calm in the face of danger; while NASA engineers were completing the final checks for what they felt would be the most difficult flight yet—*Faith 7* was to circle the earth 22 times—Cooper was sound asleep in the capsule atop the rocket. He managed to stay awake throughout the 34-

John Glenn became the first American to orbit the earth on February 20, 1962, when he completed three circuits around the planet during the Mercury-Atlas 6 mission. Glenn, gazing at the earth through the window of Friendship 7, provided America with the first detailed descriptions of the planet as seen from outer space. The view, Glenn said simply, was "beautiful."

John Glenn receives a visit from President John F. Kennedy at Cape Canaveral following the flight of Friendship 7. *Glenn was hailed as an American hero for his feat of circling the earth three times and bringing his spacecraft down safely despite various mechanical difficulties.*

hour flight, however, and when the automatic control system broke down shortly before reentry, Cooper calmly brought *Faith 7* down through the atmosphere by hand, while telling mission control over the radio that he intended to land the craft right on the deck of the prime recovery ship (he splashed down only 700 yards away). With that, Project Mercury was over.

The Soviet Vostok program was coming to an end as well, but Chief Designer Korolyov had one more surprise to spring on NASA. On June 14, 1963, *Vostok 5* was launched. On June 16, *Vostok 6* went up. This was not surprising in itself, after the *Vostok 3–Vostok 4* joint mission. The surprise came when the Soviet Union released the name of the pilot of *Vostok 6*: Valentina Tereshkova. The cosmonaut was a woman!

Valentina Tereshkova was born on March 6, 1937, on the collective farm of Maslennikovo, about 190 miles northeast of Moscow. Her father, a tractor driver, was killed in combat during World War II. In 1945, her family moved to the city of Yaroslavl, and at the age of 16, Valentina began working in the Yaroslavl Tire Factory while continuing her education at night. In 1955, she transferred to the Krasnyi Perekop Textile Mill, where she operated a loom, and by 1961, she was a graduate cotton-spinning technologist. She was also head of the Textile Mill Workers Parachute Club and secretary of the local Komsomol (Young Communist League) chapter.

Following *Vostok 1*, Valentina, like many girls and young women in the Soviet Union, dreamed of becoming a cosmonaut. In the United States at that time, there were probably girls who dreamed of becoming astronauts, but their dreams, unlike the John Glenn–inspired dreams of American boys, had little chance of becoming reality. In the Soviet Union, however, officials had already begun considering sending up a woman cosmonaut. After *Vostok 2*, Valentina wrote to the Supreme Soviet in Moscow and volunteered for cosmonaut service. On February 16, 1962,

she and four other young women were selected. After undergoing the same training program as the male cosmonauts, Valentina Tereshkova was chosen to fly Vostok 6, the final mission of the Vostok program. Tereshkova's flight was supposed to last only one day, but she adapted so well that the chief designer decided to extend it to nearly three. She returned safely to earth late on the morning of June 19. She had spent more time in space (2 days, 22 hours) and completed more orbits (48) than any American astronaut up to that point. It would take NASA 20 years to catch up with this particular accomplishment of the Soviet space program.

NASA officials congratulate astronaut Gordon Cooper on the deck of the Kearsarge after the successful completion of his 36-hour Mercury-Atlas 9 flight, the final mission of Project Mercury.

"There Are More Things in Heaven and Earth"

I believe that this nation should commit itself to achieving the goal, before this decade is out, of landing a man on the moon and returning him safely to earth." With these words, spoken on May 25, 1961, to a joint session of Congress, President John F. Kennedy seized the initiative from the Soviet Union's space program and, in effect, upped the ante in the space race. By setting such an ambitious goal for NASA—the moon itself—Kennedy had put the United States in the position of front-runner. Despite the comparative achievements of the American and Soviet space programs, to the world at large, it no longer seemed that NASA was struggling to keep up with the Soviets; instead, the Soviets were chasing NASA on a race to the moon. It was a brilliant stroke for Kennedy, but like any gamble, it was risky as well. Failure to attain the moon first—if it could be attained at all—would result in irreparable damage to U.S. prestige. And the dangers inherent in space exploration would be multiplied and intensified by the difficulty of the task and by the rush to meet Kennedy's end-of-the-decade deadline. As Gemini and Apollo astronaut Michael Collins put it, "There were *so* many ways in which we could screw up, *so* many possibilities for error, that hardly an hour would pass without a fresh opportunity for disaster."

NASA began gearing up for the race to the moon. The gigantic NASA Manned Space Center was built near

On May 25, 1961, President John F. Kennedy addressed a joint session of Congress and declared, "I believe this nation should commit itself to achieving the goal, before this decade is out, of landing a man on the moon and returning him safely to earth." Project Mercury had been the first step toward realizing this goal; Project Gemini would be the second.

Houston, Texas, and Project Gemini was initiated. Project Gemini would represent the long backstretch in the space race, connecting the first laps of the race—Project Mercury—with the homestretch, Project Apollo. With Project Mercury, the atmosphere had been breached and outer space penetrated. Before a trip to the moon could be attempted, NASA would have to produce the hardware, train the astronauts, and develop the know-how needed to sustain a long-term trip through outer space. In particular, problems associated with multiple-astronaut crews would have to be addressed, and docking (the joining of two spacecraft in outer space) and EVA (extravehicular activity, or space walk) techniques would have to be developed and perfected. These were the main obstacles faced by the thousands of NASA employees in Houston as Project Gemini got rolling.

Soviet chief designer Korolyov was feeling the heat of the space race as well. Premier Nikita Khrushchev was pressuring him to keep the Soviet program ahead of NASA's. In particular, Khrushchev hoped to upstage NASA in the area of long-duration multipassenger flights and space walks. The first manned Gemini flight was slated for launch in early 1965; Korolyov's Voskhod (Sunrise) project got into space six months earlier. The crew of the first multipassenger spaceflight consisted of Vladimir Komarov, Konstantin Feoktistov, and Boris Yegorov. Mission Commander Komarov, like all the previous cosmonauts, was a military pilot. Feoktistov and Yegorov, however, were the first nonpilots to fly in space. Konstantin Feoktistov was a member of Korolyov's design bureau, and Yegorov, the first physician in space, was the son of a prominent Moscow brain surgeon and a graduate of the Moscow First Medical Institute. Cosmonaut Yegorov's specialty was the vestibular, or balance-sensing, organ of the inner ear.

Voskhod 1 was a modified Vostok and was in many ways

NASA officials confer in the mission control center at NASA's Manned Space Center, Houston, Texas. Construction on the massive installation began in 1961 as part of NASA's drive to put an American on the moon.

identical to the Vostok vehicles. Most of Korolyov's modifications were centered around making the crew cabin large enough for three cosmonauts rather than one. (It was a tight fit; the cosmonauts themselves could not wear space suits because there was not enough room inside the

The two ill-fated heroes of the early Soviet space program. Yury Gagarin (in uniform), the most famous and beloved of the cosmonauts, was killed in a jet-airplane crash in 1968. Vladimir Komarov was killed in 1967 when his Soyuz capsule crash-landed.

cabin to accommodate three men in bulky pressure suits. Instead, they wore blue shirts, brown trousers, and light-weight communications caps and were careful to make sure that the hatch remained fully closed so that no loss of cabin pressure could occur.) *Voskhod 1* also had a more powerful booster rocket; the SL-4 could propel the 3 cosmonauts into an orbit 60 to 120 miles higher than that of their predecessors.

Voskhod 1 achieved a successful lift-off on October 12, 1964. After establishing orbit, Feoktistov tested the new spacecraft's systems, photographed the earth, and conducted astronomical observations. Yegorov studied the reactions of Komarov and Feoktistov to orbital flight and conducted experiments on the effects of weightlessness on the inner ear. Although the mission was going smoothly, after only a day in orbit, Korolyov ordered *Voskhod 1* to return to earth. Komarov objected, stating that they wanted to remain in space longer. Komarov's reluctance to return is understandable considering the problems he had overcome in getting himself aboard a spaceflight in the first place. During the initial cosmonaut training, Soviet physicians discovered that Komarov had a hernia. Surgery was needed, and the doctors feared that Komarov would have to drop out of the cosmonaut corps because he would be unable to withstand the strenuous physical activity required. However, the determined Komarov recovered within six months and convinced the doctors to let him rejoin the space program.

A short time later, doctors detected another medical problem during a centrifuge run. The unlucky Komarov had a systolic heart murmur, a condition caused by an extra contraction of the ventricles. Once again stripped of flight status, Komarov, much like NASA's Deke Slayton, spent the next several weeks visiting the leading heart specialists in an attempt to obtain confirmation that his irregular heartbeat would not cause any problems during spaceflight. Komarov won his argument and, for a second time, was readmitted to the cosmonaut team.

And now, after he had finally made it into outer space, Korolyov was telling him to come back down after only a day! In the ensuing conversation between the chief designer and the mission commander, Korolyov responded to Komarov's request for an explanation by quoting from William Shakespeare's *Hamlet*: "There are more things in Heaven and Earth, Horatio, than are dreamt of in your philosophy." Komarov interpreted this cryptic remark as a reference to the situation on earth—and in Moscow in particular—rather than in heaven. Changes in the Central Committee were imminent, and subsequent changes in the space program were perhaps imminent as well. There was a chance, Komarov knew, that the Soviet space effort might even be brought to a halt. So, after only 16 orbits and 24 hours in space, Komarov brought *Voskhod 1* back down to the Soviet Union. A day later, it was announced that Premier Khrushchev had been deposed; Leonid Brezhnev was the new first secretary of the Central Committee of the Communist party. But Korolyov and Komarov soon learned, to their relief, that the Soviet space program would continue as planned—for the time being, at least.

Voskhod 2 carried only two cosmonauts, but one of them would be the first human to venture outside a spacecraft during orbit. *Voskhod 2* lifted off from Baikonur on March 18, 1965, with cosmonauts Pavel Belyayev and Aleksey Leonov aboard. Mission Commander Belyayev was a Soviet naval fighter pilot; Leonov was a parachute instructor in the Soviet air force. Belyayev would remain inside the cabin while Leonov attempted the first EVA. During the initial orbit, Leonov began preparations for his space walk. *Voskhod 2* carried a tubular, inflatable air lock outside the cabin hatch. To exit the cabin, Leonov first inflated the air lock. Then he opened the inner hatch separating the cabin and the air lock and crawled inside the air lock.

Belyayev closed the hatch behind Leonov, who then depressurized the air lock, which would allow him to open the outer hatch. As *Voskhod 2* finished its first orbit and passed over the Caspian Sea, Leonov opened the final hatch and floated out: a pressure-suited infant delivered into a black void. On earth, his progress was observed via a television camera mounted on the back of the retro-rocket housing.

Connected to the mother ship and sustained within his pressure suit (because there were only two cosmonauts on *Voskhod 2*, there was enough room for both of them to wear suits) by an umbilical line, Leonov floated alongside the spacecraft, man and vehicle hurtling around the earth at about 15,000 miles per hour. Astounded Soviet and European television audiences watched the cosmonaut twirling on the end of the umbilical. After about 10 minutes, Belyayev informed Leonov that it was time for him to crawl back into the air lock and return to the cabin. But when Leonov attempted to reenter the air lock, he found to his horror that he could not fit. His space suit had ballooned in the vacuum of space, and he could not fit through the hatch. He struggled to get inside and began to feel weak and tired; moving in the pressure suit was extremely arduous. Twice Leonov reduced the pressure in his space suit. Finally, with one last, desperate effort, he forced himself into the narrow tube. After closing the outer hatch and repressurizing the air lock, he opened the inner hatch to rejoin a relieved Belyayev. Leonov, exhausted and soaked in perspiration, was never so glad to see another human face. (Nor was Belyayev; if the space walker had been unable to get back in through the hatch, Belyayev would have had to cut his comrade loose before he could attempt reentry into the earth's atmosphere.)

There were more tribulations ahead for the two cosmonauts. The next day, at the end of orbit 16, the retro-rocket was supposed to fire for reentry. At the designated time for retrofire, however, instruments showed that *Voskhod 2* was not properly aligned. Belyayev took manual control of the spacecraft and fired the retro-rocket at the end of the next orbit. Their angle was a little too steep as they hit the atmosphere, and consequently the heat generated during reentry was so intense that all of the spacecraft's radio antennae burned away. Because of the postponed reentry, they found themselves descending under their parachute into a harsh, snow-covered, heavily forested area in the Ural Mountains, which form a natural border between the Soviet Union and central Asia. They landed more than 1,000 miles away from the designated touchdown site. And with the radio antennae gone, they could not contact mission control to report their whereabouts.

Belyayev and Leonov crawled out of the capsule to take a look around. The terrain was so desolate they might as well have landed on the moon. It was bitterly cold, and it would get even colder when the sun went down. They set up a radio beacon and built a fire. About three hours later they heard a search plane circling overhead. A short time after that, a helicopter dropped some supplies, but it could not land because the terrain was too rugged. As night closed in, the cosmonauts heard the howling of wolves and saw the animals' gray, shadowy figures lurking in the woods nearby. Eventually, the wolves forced them to abandon what little warmth their fire provided and return to the capsule. They spent the night huddled inside *Voskhod 2*, shivering, listening to the wolves, and wishing they were still in orbit. At daybreak, recovery teams—on skis—finally reached the two disconsolate cosmonauts, and they all skied down from the landing site to more hospitable environs.

Voskhod 2 was the last of that program. Despite the occasional misadventures, Voskhod was yet another success for the Soviet space effort. The two Voskhod missions provided the Soviets with experience in multipassenger

Aleksey Leonov moves through the air lock of Voskhod 2 *as he prepares to begin the first space walk. Although Leonov experienced several hair-raising minutes when he had trouble squeezing back through the hatch, his EVA (extravehicular activity) was deemed a success.*

spaceflight and allowed them to engage in extravehicular activity before NASA. As Korolyov turned his attention to the next Soviet program, called Soyuz, NASA was still behind him in the space race. But the Americans were gaining quickly, and Project Gemini would enable NASA to finally surge ahead of the chief designer.

"Eight Days or Bust"

The NASA project that would bridge the gap between Mercury's relatively short forays into near-earth space and Apollo's lunar voyages was named Project Gemini after the twins in the zodiac; the Gemini spacecraft would carry two astronauts instead of one. The Gemini astronauts were trained to concentrate on orbital rendezvous and docking techniques, EVA procedures, and long-duration space-flight research. NASA recruited 23 new astronauts for Project Gemini; some members of the original 7 would also fly the Gemini spacecraft.

McDonnell Aircraft, builders of the Mercury capsule, also built the Gemini capsule. Outwardly, Gemini resembled its predecessor. Like Mercury, it was bell shaped. Gemini was considerably larger, however: 18.75 feet long and 10 feet wide at its base, and weighing 8,000 pounds. The crew compartment was about 50 percent larger than the Mercury cabin. As far as maneuverability was concerned, Gemini was much more sophisticated than Mercury. Astronauts would be able to do much more actual piloting on Gemini flights, rather than simply riding along as a passenger. (The astronauts were quite pleased about this.) Gemini was the first spacecraft that could translate, or change from one orbit to another in space (Mercury could change its attitude, but not its orbit). And, boosted into orbit by the air force Titan II missile, it could achieve altitudes far beyond the reach of Vostok, Mercury, or Voskhod.

NASA's Agena target vehicle as seen from the Gemini spacecraft during rendezvous and docking exercises. The Agena is about 75 feet from the Gemini, and the tether connecting the 2 vehicles has just been jettisoned. The docking and rendezvous techniques necessary for a flight to the moon were first explored during Project Gemini.

The Gemini astronauts. In the back row, from left to right are Elliot M. See, James A. McDivitt, James A. Lovell, Edward H. White II, and Thomas P. Stafford. In the front row, from left to right are Charles Conrad, Frank Borman, Neil A. Armstrong, and John W. Young.

Crew designations aboard Gemini flights were command pilot and pilot. Veteran astronaut Gus Grissom was command pilot on the first manned Gemini flight, Gemini-Titan III. His pilot was U.S. Navy test pilot John W. Young. Because of his brush with a watery death following his Mercury-Redstone 4 splashdown, Grissom wanted to name his Gemini spacecraft *Molly Brown*, after "Unsink-

able" Molly Brown, one of the survivors of the *Titanic*.
NASA officials thought the name lacked dignity but found
Grissom's second choice—*Titanic*—even more objection-
able. Officially, there would be no name for the vehicle
other than *Gemini 3*. Unofficially, however, the spacecraft
was referred to as *Molly Brown*.

The Gemini-Titan III mission began at 9:24 A.M. on

March 23, 1965. Five minutes, 34 seconds after lift-off, Grissom and Young were in orbit. The astronauts' main objective for Gemini-Titan III was to check out the maneuvering capabilities of their new spacecraft. On the initial circuit of the earth, Grissom fired the maneuvering rockets to lower *Gemini 3*'s orbit. This was the first time a manned spacecraft had altered its flight path. In preparation for retrofire, on the third orbit, Grissom lowered

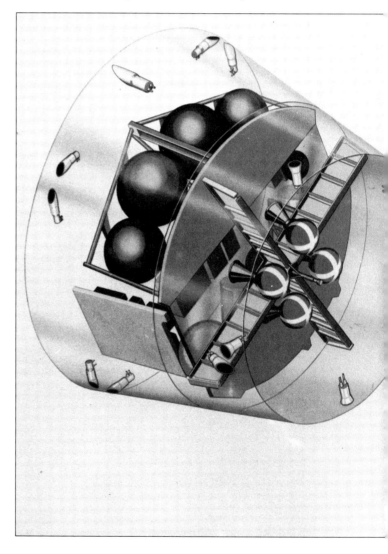

the spacecraft's perigee to 52 miles. This way, even if the retro-rockets failed to fire, Grissom and Young would be assured of an eventual reentry by way of the earth's gravitational pull. After 3 orbits, *Gemini 3* achieved a successful reentry and landed on the ocean about 58 miles short of the predicted landing point. Riding 5-foot swells, Grissom and Young had to wait for about 30 minutes before recovery teams reached them. Grissom, perhaps

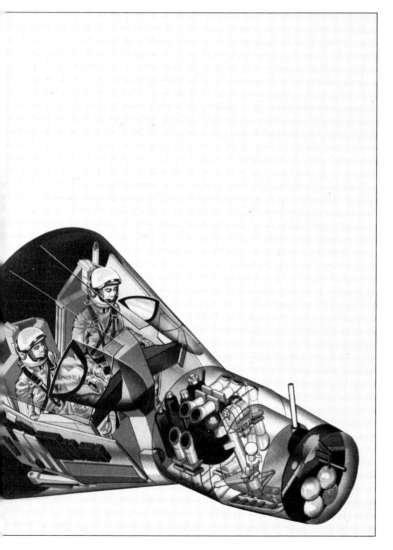

The Gemini spacecraft and command module. Although the Gemini was much larger than the Mercury and carried two passengers instead of one, the astronauts had to endure extended periods at extremely close quarters.

Edward H. White II becomes the first American to egress a spacecraft while in orbit, June 3, 1965. He is attached to Gemini *4 by an umbilical line. Behind him is the earth.*

recalling his last splashdown, became seasick. Aside from that and a slight controversy that arose when Young revealed that he had smuggled a corned beef sandwich into space, the first manned Gemini was deemed a success.

Project Gemini maintained a rapid launch rate, with a flight scheduled about every three months. Gemini-Titan IV was launched on June 3, 1965. This was the first flight to be controlled from the Manned Space Center in Houston, rather than from Cape Canaveral. Two new astronauts flew *Gemini 4*: James A. McDivitt was the command pilot; the pilot was Edward H. White II. (After Grissom's *Molly Brown* request, in order to discourage high-spirited astronauts from choosing names that were thought to be a little too colorful, NASA officials began naming the spacecraft by their project name, *Gemini*, plus the mission, or flight number, 4, 5, and so on.) White had been given a special assignment; he was going to attempt the first American EVA. This came as a surprise to almost everyone but McDivitt, White, and the highest-ranking NASA officials; the decision that White would attempt a space walk had not been made until shortly before the flight was underway. The reaction of most people to the announcement was adequately represented by Pat Collins, the wife of astronaut Michael Collins: "My God," she exclaimed, "he's *getting out!*"

About 4 hours after lift-off, wearing a helmet with a gold-coated visor to shield his eyes from the intense solar radiation, protected by a pressure suit (White's suit had a restraining mesh in order to prevent the suit from ballooning like Leonov's), and connected to the spacecraft by a 25-foot-long umbilical that contained the oxygen supply hose, communications lines, and a mechanical tether, White opened the hatch and floated into space. The astronaut was also carrying something that the cosmonaut spacewalker did not have—the hand-held maneuvering unit (HHMU). The HHMU's miniature thrusters, responding to the astronaut's hand movements, allowed him to zip around outside the spacecraft like Buck Rogers. Ed White used the instrument until it ran out of fuel. An exuberant White then found himself clutching the rear end of *Gemini 4*, 100 miles above the earth and traveling at 17,500 miles per hour. Mission control was telling him to get back inside the cabin, but White was having so much fun that he wanted to stay outside a little longer. Finally, using the umbilical as a rope, he walked back across the length of the spacecraft and, reluctantly, climbed in through the hatch. White's EVA had lasted 21 minutes. The 2 astronauts settled in for the rest of their 4-day flight, which they concluded without incident after 62 orbits.

The objective of the next mission, Gemini-Titan V, was to establish a manned spaceflight duration record of

A photograph of the Baja California peninsula taken by a member of the Gemini-Titan V crew during their record-setting eight-day flight, from August 21 to August 29, 1965. Altitude as well as endurance records were being set during Project Gemini; with each new altitude mark, the earth, as seen from the windows of the spacecraft, grew smaller.

eight days and to see how the astronauts responded, physically and psychologically, to being confined within the tiny capsule for an extended period. (Michael Collins, who would spend three days aboard a Gemini spacecraft, compared it to being stuck inside the front seat of a Volkswagen for three days—along with somebody else.) Mercury veteran Gordon Cooper was the command pilot; rookie Pete Conrad would sit in the traditional right-hand seat of the

Command Pilot Frank Borman and Pilot James Lovell, wearing new lightweight space suits designed for long-duration flights, walk to the launch-tower elevator on the morning of December 7, 1965. Blast-off is about two hours away. The "suitcases" they are carrying are portable oxygen units.

copilot. Cooper had designed a patch for the flight; it showed a covered wagon bearing the slogan Eight Days or Bust. At first, it seemed that it was going to be "bust" rather than eight days. Problems with the fuel cells that generated electricity for the spacecraft became apparent during the sixth orbit, and NASA considered terminating the flight. But after the astronauts turned off all but the most essential equipment, NASA decided to let it continue for one day. On the second day, the power situation improved slightly, and NASA decided to extend the flight for another 24 hours. In this manner, Cooper, Conrad, and NASA managed to coax an 8-day flight out of their spacecraft, circling the globe 120 times and traveling a distance of 3,312,993 miles. By the time they splashed down, on August 29, the two astronauts were exhausted, unshaven, bedraggled, and a little irritable, but they had proved that astronauts could function effectively while enclosed within a small capsule for an extended period of time.

The only major objectives of the Gemini program that still had not been attempted were orbital rendezvous and docking. These would prove to be the most difficult—and perilous—operations that the Gemini astronauts engaged in. They were also essential to the success of the Apollo lunar program. During a trip to the moon, there would be several crucial rendezvous and docking episodes. For example, once the Apollo was in orbit around the moon, the lunar module would separate from the command module. While the command module remained in orbit, the lunar module would land on the moon. The lunar module would then have to blast off from the moon and rendezvous and dock with the command module for the long ride home. A mistake or mishap during this sequence might leave astronauts as permanent lunar residents. It was up to the Gemini astronauts to prove that rendezvous and docking could be accomplished in space. The difficult nature of rendezvous and docking missions became apparent immediately. Docking missions required another, unmanned spacecraft for use as a target vehicle. For the Gemini missions, NASA decided to use an Agena rocket as the target vehicle. The Agena, originally developed as an upper stage for use with the Thor and Atlas rockets, was modified for the Gemini missions. A docking cone was attached to the Agena's nose; during the docking, the nose of a Gemini spacecraft would fit neatly into the Agena docking cone, and three latches would lock the two ships together, making them, in effect, one spaceship. For the Gemini-Titan VI mission, the unmanned Agena would be launched into orbit first, boosted by an Atlas rocket; the two astronauts aboard *Gemini 6*—Wally Schirra and Tom Stafford—would go up about an hour and a half later. In theory, they would then rendezvous and dock with the Agena in outer space. In theory.

On the morning of October 25, 1965, Schirra and Stafford, snug within their Gemini capsule atop the behemoth Titan booster, waited for word that the Agena target vehicle had been launched. They were to follow 90 minutes later. Six minutes after the Agena Atlas took off, ground control stopped receiving data, and then air force radar technicians found themselves tracking numerous objects where only one had been a moment before. The Agena Atlas had blown up. With no target to pursue, the disgusted Schirra and Stafford climbed out of *Gemini 6*. NASA then displayed one of its strengths—the ability to improvise and turn failure into success. A bold new plan was announced: *Gemini 6* would be launched, but instead of an Agena rendezvous, Schirra and Stafford would rendezvous with the manned *Gemini 7*. The two Gemini spacecraft would not be able to dock, but they would be able to rendezvous. Gemini-Titan VII was a two-week mission originally scheduled for late December 1965. For *Gemini 6* to rendezvous with *Gemini 7* would require a herculean effort by the launch team. Still, the mission was worth attempting.

Gemini 7, with astronauts Frank Borman and James

Lovell aboard, was launched successfully on December 4, 1965. The Titan booster inserted the spacecraft into an orbit with a perigee of 100.28 miles and an apogee of 203.66 miles. Less than 24 hours after *Gemini 7* lifted off, Schirra and Stafford were once again strapped into the *Gemini 6* capsule (now called *Gemini 6A*), which was once again pointed to the sky atop the Titan booster. The countdown began: "Six, five, four, three, two, one . . ." Nothing. Nothing happened. Command Pilot Schirra was now faced with one of the life-or-death decisions that astronauts are frequently forced to make, and he had, literally, about a second to make it in. In his book *Carrying the Fire*, astronaut Michael Collins described the situation: "They [Schirra and Stafford] had about a second to review two scenarios. (1) the engines for some reason had shut down after lift-off, and they were now on the brink of disaster and would either settle back down or topple over, requiring immediate ejection to avoid the ensuing holocaust; (2) the engines had shut down the instant *before* lift-off, in which case they were still firmly bolted to the launchpad and could stay put unless some new danger developed." Schirra picked scenario 2, and it turned out that he made the right choice—the engines had indeed shut down just before lift-off. If he and Stafford had ejected needlessly, the flight would have been scrubbed, a major setback for NASA, especially after the failure of the Agena. Instead, mission Gemini-Titan VI-A was saved, and a third launch attempt, to the relief of Stafford and Schirra, was successful.

Five hours and 46 minutes after launch, *Gemini 6A* was within 120 feet of *Gemini 7*. The world's first controlled rendezvous in space had occurred. The two spacecraft flew to within a foot of each other, then flew in formation for four orbits before drifting apart. Schirra and Stafford returned to earth the next day; Borman and Lovell remained in orbit until December 18, setting another spaceflight duration record of two weeks.

Gemini-Titan VIII inherited the docking attempt. *Gemini* 8 blasted off on March 16, 1966—the 40th anniversary of the world's first liquid-fuel rocket launch by Robert Goddard—with Command Pilot Neil Armstrong and Pilot David Scott at the controls. The unmanned Agena had gone up without any problems 101 minutes earlier. After chasing the target vehicle around the earth for six hours, Armstrong and Scott reported that they were within 150 feet of the Agena. Thirty-four minutes later, Armstrong gently nudged *Gemini* 8's nose into the Agena docking cone, and the two spacecraft were one. The first-ever docking was "a real smoothie," Armstrong reported. He did not know that the most harrowing 10 minutes in the history of NASA (up to that point) were about to begin.

About 27 minutes after docking, and while out of range of any ground stations, the spacecraft suddenly began to spin and roll. Armstrong, thinking that the Agena was causing the roll, separated *Gemini* 8 from the Agena. This move backfired; there was nothing wrong with the Agena, but one of the *Gemini* 8's orbital maneuvering thrusters was stuck in the on position and was firing continuously. Now, without the stabilizing weight of the Agena, *Gemini* 8 began to roll faster and faster. When *Gemini* 8 came within range of the tracking ship *Coastal Sentry Quebec*, flight controllers received a signal indicating that the vehicles were no longer docked. They asked what was happening and received a startling reply from a nervous Scott: "We have serious problems here . . . we're tumbling end over end up here."

The situation was serious; *Gemini* 8 was tumbling at a rate approaching *one revolution per second*. Armstrong and Scott were getting dizzy and their vision was blurry; soon they would become disoriented. Things were on the verge of getting completely out of control. Mission Commander Armstrong, like Wally Schirra, needed to make a quick decision. He shut off the orbital maneuvering rockets and then activated the reentry control system (RCS) thrusters.

Using these thrusters to counteract the spinning, he quickly regained control of *Gemini 8*. NASA then decided to abort the rest of the flight and bring the astronauts down immediately. Reentry occurred nowhere near the predetermined point, so *Gemini 8* splashed down on the Pacific Ocean instead of the Atlantic. Still dizzy, but safe, Armstrong and Scott were picked up by a navy destroyer.

Despite *Gemini 8*'s tumbling episode, NASA was happy with the successful docking. True, there had been problems, but they had been dealt with and overcome and, most important, NASA and its astronauts had learned from them. There would be four more Gemini missions before the year was out; astronauts would continue their attempts to master EVA, rendezvous, and docking techniques, and NASA would continue to accumulate and process the data needed to put an American on the moon. With the splashdown of *Gemini 12* on November 15, 1966, Project Gemini officially came to an end, and NASA turned its attention toward Project Apollo and the moon. Confidence was at an all-time high.

Gemini 7 and Gemini 6A seem almost close enough to touch during their December 1965 rendezvous. But it was not until the following mission, Gemini-Titan 8, that NASA would accomplish an actual outer space docking.

The White Room

In the early afternoon of January 27, 1967, at the Kennedy Space Center (formerly Cape Canaveral) in Florida, astronauts Gus Grissom, Ed White, and Roger Chaffee, the men chosen to fly the first Apollo mission, finished a brief lunch, suited up, walked through the White Room, which connected the service tower to the spacecraft, and climbed laboriously into the *Apollo I* command module, sitting atop its 363-foot-tall Saturn booster rocket. NASA technicians sealed the hatch behind the astronauts, and another long day of testing began. For every hour in space, there were thousands of hours of such methodical flight rehearsal and systems checks.

About five hours later, at 6:31 P.M., the crew in the White Room heard the voice of Gus Grissom yelling over the radio, "Fire!" Technicians scrambled as the astronaut's voice grew urgent, then desperate: "We've got a fire in the cockpit. . . . We've got a bad fire . . . let's get out . . . open 'er up . . . we're burning up." These were the last words from the command module. Seconds later, fire and smoke exploded into the White Room, driving back the rescuers who were trying to get to the hatch. Five minutes passed as they battled the heat and smoke and tried to undo the hatch. When the hatch was finally opened, it was only to reveal a horrific scene: The interior of the command module had been badly burned in the intense heat, and Grissom, White, and Chaffee slumped dead in

The charred hull of the Apollo command module that became a death trap for astronauts Gus Grissom, Edward H. White II, and Roger Chaffee when a flash fire erupted inside the capsule during preflight testing on January 27, 1967.

their charred space suits.

The White Room catastrophe shocked NASA and the American public deeply. The kind of grim bureaucratic process that would follow the *Challenger* disaster 19 years later was set in motion. The Apollo Review Board, like the commission that investigated the *Challenger* explosion, found fault with both NASA and the independent contractors who built the Apollo command module. It was determined that a short circuit in the *Apollo I* wiring caused a fire that ignited explosively in the pure-oxygen atmosphere of the cockpit. Because of the sealed hatch, there had been no quick escape route for the astronauts— once the fire started, they had no chance.

Nineteen sixty-seven was a bad year for the Soviet space program as well. The Soviet program and NASA had paralleled one another in the race to accomplish outer-space firsts, and they continued to do so in an almost uncanny manner. Little more than three months after the White Room fire, the Soviets launched their answer to Apollo— *Soyuz I.* The new spacecraft was piloted by veteran cosmonaut Vladimir Komarov. After a successful 17-orbit flight, Komarov attempted reentry. During its descent, *Soyuz I*'s parachute did not deploy correctly and failed to slow the spacecraft's fall sufficiently. The impact with the ground killed Komarov.

These events marked turning points for both space programs. The space race was over. The Soviets had hoped that their Soyuz program would challenge NASA's Apollo effort in the race to the moon, but following the death of Komarov and a succession of problems with their newly developed large boosters, the Soviets began concentrating on long-term, manned orbital operations. Their pioneering efforts in establishing and maintaining space stations were far less spectacular than NASA's quest for the moon, but no less important. Should an attempt at an extended space voyage be made by either country—a manned flight to Mars, for example—the experience of the Soviets in

Scenes from NASA's future: Lunar module Intrepid, *with astronauts Charles Conrad and Alan Bean aboard, comes in for a landing on the moon's Ocean of Storms, in November 1969.*

maintaining healthy humans in outer space for long periods will be invaluable.

With the deaths of Grissom, White, and Chaffee providing tragic proof of the dangers involved in space exploration, it would have been easy for NASA to back off Kennedy's end-of-the-decade deadline. It is a testament to the resiliency of NASA, its astronauts, and the American public that the White Room fire did not permanently derail the moon effort. More important, however, it is evidence of the fundamental need that propels earth rockets into outer space. After the flight of Yury Gagarin, humans were no longer an earthbound species; they had emerged from the cocoon of the planet's atmosphere and were taking their first, tentative look around. After Gagarin it was inevitable—politics, crashes, and deaths notwithstanding—that men and women would return to outer space again and again. And the moon, like a beacon, waited in the night sky.

Further Reading

Anderson, Frank W. *Orders of Magnitude: A History of NACA and NASA 1915–1980.* Washington, DC: National Aeronautics and Space Administration, 1981.

Braun, Wernher von. *Space Travel: A History.* New York: Harper & Row, 1985.

Cassutt, Michael. *Who's Who in Space.* Boston: G. K. Hall, 1987.

Clark, Philip. *The Soviet Manned Space Program.* New York: Crown, 1988.

Collins, Michael. *Carrying the Fire.* New York: Farrar, Straus & Giroux, 1974.

———. *Liftoff: The Story of America's Adventure in Space.* New York: Grove Press, 1988.

Cooper, Gordon L., and John H. Glenn, et al. *We Seven: By the Astronauts Themselves.* New York: Simon & Schuster, 1962.

Crouch, Tom D. *The National Aeronautics and Space Administration.* New York: Chelsea House, 1990.

Gatland, Kenneth. *Manned Spacecraft.* New York: Macmillan, 1976.

Hacker, Barton C., and James M. Grimwood. *On the Shoulders of Titans.* Washington, DC: National Aeronautics and Space Administration, 1977.

Harvey, Brian. *Race into Space*. Chichester, England: Ellis Horwood Ltd., 1988.

Hurt, Harry, III. *For All Mankind*. New York: Atlantic Monthly Press, 1988.

Krieger, F. J. *Behind the Sputniks*. Washington, DC: Public Affairs Press, 1958.

McDougall, Walter A. *Heavens and the Earth: A Political History of the Space Age*. New York: Basic Books, 1985.

Mallan, Lloyd. *Men, Rockets, and Space Rats*. New York: Julian Messner, 1955.

National Aeronautics and Space Administration. *The First Twenty-five Years: 1958–1983*. Washington, DC: Government Printing Office, 1983.

Oberg, James E. *Red Star in Orbit*. New York: Random House, 1981.

Riabchikov, Evgeny. *Russians in Space*. Garden City, NY: Doubleday, 1971.

Simons, David G., and Don A. Schanche. *Man High*. New York: Doubleday, 1960.

Swenson, Lloyd S., James M. Grimwood, and Charles C. Alexander. *This New Ocean: A History of Project Mercury*. Washington, DC: National Aeronautics and Space Administration, 1966.

Wolfe, Tom. *The Right Stuff*. New York: Farrar, Straus & Giroux, 1979.

Chronology

Entries in roman type refer to events directly related to space travel; events in italics refer to important historical and cultural events of the time.

1945	*Allies achieve victory in Europe; Germany is divided into American and Soviet spheres of influence; the cold war begins*
June 1948	Albert, a rhesus monkey, is the first of many animals to be used in V-2 rocket experiments in space; he dies shortly after lift-off
1955	Project Manhigh begins testing the effects of an outer-space environment on animals and humans, using high-altitude balloon flights
Oct. 1957	Soviets launch first man-made earth satellite, *Sputnik 1*
July 1958	Congress passes the National Aeronautics and Space Act, creating the National Aeronautics and Space Administration (NASA); Projects Mercury (U.S.) and Vostok (USSR) are created to conduct manned spaceflights
April 1959	Seven jet-fighter pilots are chosen as the first astronauts for Project Mercury; shortly thereafter the Soviets choose the first six cosmonauts
1960	*John F. Kennedy elected 35th president of the United States*
1961	*Berlin Wall constructed;* Yuri Gagarin, on *Vostok 1,* becomes the first man to orbit the earth; Alan Shepard, a month later, becomes the first American in space

1962	*Cuban missile crisis escalates the cold war;* John Glenn becomes the first American to orbit the earth; Soviet Adrian "Iron Man" Nikolayev, in *Vostok 3,* completes 64 orbits in 96 hours, during which his ship rendezvouses with another Soviet spacecraft, *Vostok 4*
June 1963	Valentina Tereshkova becomes the first woman in space, circling the earth 48 times
Nov. 1963	*John F. Kennedy is assassinated; Lyndon Johnson becomes president*
Oct. 1964	*Voskhod 1 is the first spaceflight to carry more than one person; Nikita Khrushchev is deposed as Soviet leader; Leonid Brezhnev assumes control*
1965	Soviet Aleksey Leonov becomes the first human to walk in space; Project Gemini proceeds with Gus Grissom and John Young aboard *Gemini 3;* astronauts Gordon Cooper and Pete Conrad establish manned spaceflight endurance record of 8 days while circling the earth 120 times; *Gemini 6A* and *Gemini 7* rendezvous in space, flying within one foot of each other
March 1966	*Gemini 8* completes first docking mission in space
Jan. 1967	Astronauts Grissom, Ed White, and Roger Chaffee become the first casualties of the space program as *Apollo 1* catches fire on the launching pad
April 1967	Cosmonaut Vladimir Komarov dies as the *Soyuz 1*'s parachute fails to open, ending Soviet hopes for a lunar landing

Index

Picture Credits

Gregory Kennedy is the director of the National Space Center at Alamogordo, New Mexico. A graduate of the University of Maryland, he has written several books on the subject of spaceflight, including *Vengeance Weapon Two: The V-2 Guided Missile* and *Rockets, Missiles, and Spacecraft of the National Air and Space Museum.*

William H. Goetzmann holds the Jack S. Blanton, Sr., Chair in History at the University of Texas at Austin, where he has taught for many years. The author of numerous works on American history and exploration, he won the 1967 Pulitzer and Parkman prizes for his *Exploration and Empire: The Role of the Explorer and Scientist in the Winning of the American West, 1800–1900.* With his son William N. Goetzmann, he coauthored *The West of the Imagination,* which received the Carr P. Collins Award in 1986 from the Texas Institute of Letters. His documentary television series of the same name received a blue ribbon in the history category at the American Film and Video Festival held in New York City in 1987. A recent work, *New Lands, New Men: America and the Second Great Age of Discovery,* was published in 1986 to much critical acclaim.

Michael Collins served as command module pilot on the *Apollo 11* space mission, which landed his colleagues Neil Armstrong and Buzz Aldrin on the moon. A graduate of the United States Military Academy, Collins was named an astronaut in 1963. In 1966 he piloted the *Gemini 10* mission, during which he became the third American to walk in space. The author of several books on space exploration, Collins was director of the Smithsonian Institution's National Air and Space Museum from 1971 to 1978 and is a recipient of the Presidential Medal of Freedom.

DATE			